The Adversary at Home

I believe Satan wins his most important victories in our homes—yes, in the homes of Christians too. With spiritual insight and years of personal experience, Mark Bubeck has written this book to help us win the battles for the souls of our children. Read it carefully, apply it, and share it with your friends.

—Dr. Erwin W. Lutzer
Sr. Pastor, The Moody Church

Satan's first opportunities to influence and capture people arise in the home, and parents need to be equipped for battle. I appreciate Mark Bubeck's biblical and balanced approach to spiritual warfare—an approach developed through much study and practical experience in the trenches. For the sake of the spiritual welfare of the next generation, I encourage every pastor, parent, and children's worker to read this book and take it to heart.

—Warren W. Wiersbe
Bible teacher and author of
several Bible studies including The Be Series

A battle is raging around the world, and the epicenter of that battle is family life. The battle lines have been drawn far beyond political rhetoric or cultural values. Both are included in the battle, but this battle is first and foremost a spiritual battle. Mark Bubeck presents us with biblical truth that will safely guide families through the minefields. It's a must read for every concerned father and mother. Dr. Bubeck presents spiritual insight and balanced biblical truth to help you bring up children who will be able to walk in the light in the midst of a dark and dangerous world. I pray that parents everywhere will come to understand these great principles that Mark Bubeck teaches.

—Sammy Tippit
Evangelist and director of Sammy Tippit Ministries

As a Christian counselor I highly recommend The Adversary at Home. *I found this book to be very helpful in working with families, as it addresses the problems they are facing today. All families will gain insight into how to strengthen their relationships with each other and with God. A great resource tool!*

—Dr. Jim Logan
Biblical Restoration Ministries

the *Adversary* at HOME

the *Adversary* at HOME

Protecting your child
from the evil one

MARK I. BUBECK

LIFE JOURNEY®
Bringing Home the Message for Life

COOK COMMUNICATIONS MINISTRIES
Colorado Springs, Colorado • Paris, Ontario
KINGSWAY COMMUNICATIONS LTD
Eastbourne, England

Life Journey® is an imprint of
Cook Communications Ministries, Colorado Springs, CO 80918
Cook Communications, Paris, Ontario
Kingsway Communications, Eastbourne, England

THE ADVERSARY AT HOME
© 1997 by Mark I. Bubeck

Cover Design: Jeffrey P. Barnes

First Cook Printing, 2006
Printed in Canada

1 2 3 4 5 6 7 8 9 10 Printing/Year 11 10 09 08 07 06

This book was originally published in 1997 under the title *Raising Lambs
Among Wolves,* original ISBN: 0-8024-7194-3.

ISBN-13: 978-0-7814-4308-1
ISBN-10: 0-7814-4308-3

LCCN: 2005937733

To my longtime friends and esteemed spiritual leaders,
W. and B. W.
Without their encouragement and helpful suggestions,
my writing ministry would not have existed.

Contents

Acknowledgments

My deepest appreciation goes to those friends and coun-selees who granted me permission to use their personal stories. I have taken great care to conceal the identity of each person, and wherever appropriate, constructed composite characters. Each account, however, describes the experiences of real people.

A special note of thanks is due my immediate family. My wife, Anita, each of my three daughters, and their families have contributed much to the message of this book. I find their loving trust humbling.

Introduction

And there shall be a time of trouble, such as never
was since there was a nation.... Those who are wise
shall shine like the brightness of the firmament, and
those who turn many to righteousness like the stars
forever and ever.

—Daniel 12:1, 3 NKJV

These prophetic words from an angel to Daniel are still
relevant today. The world is facing troubles like we have
never before seen. Few would disagree that the world is
descending into chaos. Children shoot other children in
schools, terrorists fly planes into buildings, and fanatics turn
themselves into human bombs.

"Trouble, such as never was ..." These prophetic thoughts
frame the message of this book. Our children are in danger.
They are, in their innocence, vulnerable to attack. Our highest priority must be to protect them and to prepare them for
life in an increasingly hostile world.

God created the family to be the foundation of civiliza-
tion, but today the home is under assault. The forces of hell

conspire to destroy it. Divorce devastates families. Gay activists aggressively promote the homosexual lifestyle as a viable life option. Society increasingly sees gay couples as simply another expression of the family and extends to them the same rights to adopt as heterosexual couples. Witchcraft and sorcery are now common fare among children's books and entertainment and even in public-school curricula.

In the midst of this increasing darkness, God has placed the Christian family. He has ordained godly parents to shine with sufficient light to turn their children to righteousness and truth. As we exercise the compassionate, protective oversight of our children, God uses us as light amid the darkness of our time and as salt to dispel corruption in the world.

The purpose of this book is to help Christian parents use the truth of God's Word to protect their children. Light overcomes darkness. To protect our children we must shine the light of truth around them.

A vital way we parents can protect our children is through prevailing prayer, which is prayer that rests on the truth of Christ's finished work. Its foundation goes deeper than mere emotions or wishful thinking. Prevailing prayer applies Christ's victories against the evil forces seeking to capture our children. (The sample prayers in this book will be helpful and will offer a practical way to use biblical truth as you pray on behalf of your children.)

Truth sets us free from the clutches of darkness; it also positively enables us to parent with freedom. Turning a child from darkness to the light of righteousness makes a parent shine "like the stars forever and ever" (Dan. 12:3 NKJV). My prayer is that God will use this book to help parents shine like stars.

Part 1

THE LEGACY
WE LEAVE

1

Footprints in the Carpet

Linn quietly entered the kitchen where her mother was busily preparing supper. A vivacious junior in college, Linn seemed unusually thoughtful. When she spoke, her eyes brimmed with tears. "Mom, is Dad still going into our rooms every night to pray for Peter and me like he did before we went to college?"

Chris was not prepared for her question. She knew Ted was dedicated to praying for their children, but her husband regarded the issue as a highly private matter. Her daughter's direct question required a straightforward response.

"Yes, he is," Chris answered, "but how did you know?"

"I saw his footprints in the carpet," Linn replied. "I never knew it would mean so much to me!" Her tears flowed freely. "I guess I'm growing up."

Parents leave "footprints" in their children's lives—footprints their children often follow. They are footprints that can lead a child away from danger and along a path of safety. We recognize, however, that all too frequently children follow a different path—one marked by a different pattern of prints.

But parents may leave behind more than footprints. We sometimes leave behind wounded children.

WOUNDS FROM OUR PARENTS

"Oh, Mommy, Mommy, please let's not go home yet!" The preschool-aged girl was pleading for help. "Please, please, Mommy! Don't make me go home yet. Daddy will yell at me. Oh, please, Mommy, please, don't make me go home. Please, Mommy, please!"

My wife overheard the words of that little child in the shopping mall. "My heart was almost torn out by her frantic, pitiful pleading," my wife confessed. "I wanted to gather her in my arms, quiet her trembling body, and reassure her of my love and protection."

The department store elevator stopped and the mother exited with her hysterical child. My wife, Anita, continued shopping, trying to forget the encounter. But the cry of a hurting child would not leave her ears. An hour later, as Anita made her way to her parked car, she again encountered the family. The little girl was still pleading, "Oh, please, Mommy, don't make me go home! Daddy will yell at me and hurt me!"

The sad countenance of the mother raised the specter of a mean-spirited and abusive husband and father who waited at home.

The wounds of abuse heal slowly. They lie just below the surface, waiting for a crisis to reopen the old scars. Healing often requires years of therapy. Parents must realize the first avenue of attack the Adversary is likely to take is through abuse. Adults often unintentionally pass the destructive effects of past abuses on to their children. Sadly, abuse may render people incapable of seeing and believing in a good and gracious heavenly Father.

Anita and I recently received a letter from a young mother whom we ministered to many years ago. Jenny reminded us of how we had been there to help during a dark time in her family life. Jenny's dad was verbally, physically, and sexually abusive to Jenny and her siblings. Jenny wrote the following in her letter.

"It's hard to believe in a loving heavenly Father when your earthly father was as cruel and abusive as ours. You are extra special, Pastor. You represented the Lord Jesus to us all. You were a good father image. Thanks for everything!"

Jenny's letter illustrates the destructive impact of abuse in a child's life. Even more powerful, though, is the ability of Jesus Christ to deliver people from the consequences of parental abuse. Jenny and her sisters are living testimonies to this truth. There is no abusive activity that exceeds God's ability to transform and heal. Parents who suffered abuse as children can recover and become bright lights that repel the Adversary who threatens their children.

God can also use our painful past for His glory. My friend Tom—a fellow pastor—was orphaned as a young child. Emotionally torn by the loss of his parents, Tom found himself in an orphanage where unfair and cruel discipline was commonplace. Yet God used Tom's ordeal to mold him into a compassionate minister. My wife and I recently met with Tom and his wife. It was wonderful to learn their adult children are faithfully serving God in full-time vocational ministry. Abusive experiences need not bring ruin to the victims of abuse.

OTHER WAYS PARENTS WOUND THEIR CHILDREN

It is possible for a parent to make mistakes that may not, strictly speaking, be what we would classify as abuse. But they are, nevertheless, pitfalls that provide opportunities for the Adversary to attack our children.

Here are a few blunders to beware:

❑ Failure to commend a child's accomplishments, implying he or she could have done better
❑ Negative comments about a child's natural appearance, intelligence, or worth
❑ Neglect of daily personal time with a child, letting work schedules and personal pursuits override such times
❑ Comparison of one child's accomplishments or behaviors to that of another
❑ Broken promises
❑ Hypocritical behavior—pretending to be something we are not
❑ Manipulation through fear ("God will punish you if you disobey.")
❑ Impatience and expressions of frustration
❑ Inability to apologize, even when you know you blew it

THE DELAYED HARVEST

When we wound our children in these ways, we leave them open to the attacks of the Adversary. They become recipients of a negative family legacy both the Old and New Testaments describe. It is the legacy of the "delayed harvest."

The apostle Paul described the delayed-harvest principle in his letter to the Galatians: "Do not be deceived, God is not mocked; for whatever a man sows, that he will also reap. For he who sows to his flesh will of the flesh reap corruption, but he who sows to the Spirit will of the Spirit reap everlasting life" (Gal. 6:7–8 NKJV).

One of life's truths is that we reap what we sow. Paul's words further remind us that others reap from the seeds we've sown. Our seed sowing will be either for good or evil. Whatever we plant in the lives of our children eventually yields a harvest. There may be a delay, but the harvest is inevitable.

The cost of sin includes more than personal guilt and harm. Our sins often lead to consequences that are far more persistent. Moses learned this very lesson.

> Now the LORD descended in the cloud and stood with him there, and proclaimed the name of the LORD. And the LORD passed before him and proclaimed, "The LORD, the LORD God, merciful and gracious, longsuffering, and abounding in goodness and truth, keeping mercy for thousands, forgiving iniquity and transgression and sin, by no means clearing the guilty, visiting the iniquity of the fathers upon the children and the children's children to the third and the fourth generation." So Moses made haste and bowed his head toward the earth, and worshiped. (Ex. 34:5–8 NKJV)

The implications of this passage are profound. Our children often harvest the fruit of what we sow—either harm or blessing. In Linn's case, her father's prayers yielded a blessing.

We have opportunity to transfer blessings from one generation to another. Exodus 20:6 speaks of God's "showing love to a thousand generations of those who love [Him] and keep [His] commandments." Godly living extends a long arm of benefit and blessing from one generation to another. The apostle Paul referred to this very principle in his words to Timothy: "I have been reminded of your sincere faith, which first lived in your grandmother Lois and in your mother Eunice and, I am persuaded, now lives in you also" (2 Tim. 1:5).

A parent's godly life, however, does not guarantee his or her children will follow the Lord or consistently resist temptation. Consider Solomon, the wise king who in his later years served God only halfheartedly. Solomon benefited from the blessing his father, David, transferred to him. After Solomon had fallen into sin near the end of his reign, God pronounced the following: "Since this is your attitude and you have not kept my covenant and my decrees, which I commanded you, I will most certainly tear the kingdom away from you and give it to one of your subordinates. Nevertheless, for the sake of David your father, I will not do it during your lifetime. I will tear it out of the hand of your son" (1 Kings 11:11–12).

Solomon's choices to sin and practice evil left little blessing to pass on to his descendants, despite the fact that he continued to benefit from his father's legacy.

Commitment to the lordship of Jesus Christ produces benefits that accrue to the generations that follow us. My brother recently showed me my great-grandfather's obituary. I read with wonder and joy two columns of text that extolled my great-grandfather's Christian character and ministry. Even though Great-grandpa Bubeck was not an ordained minister, he was a skillful presenter of the Word of God. My brothers and I, along with our extended families, continue to benefit from his godly legacy, and I now carry a copy of his obituary in my briefcase as a reminder of that legacy.

Blessings transfer from generation to generation. God has blessed my four brothers and me with Christian families who are following Christ. God has instilled in me a passion to pass on the same blessings my great-grandfather transferred to me.

A NEGATIVE HARVEST

Every parent, however, must face the fact that the delayed harvest we pass to our children may not be positive. If sin has reigned in our lives, God will visit "the iniquity of the fathers upon the children and the children's children to the third and the fourth generation" (Ex. 34:7 NKJV). Those are sobering words. No wonder Moses, upon hearing them, immediately fell on his face. He grasped the depth to which our sins affect the lives of the people who are most important to us.

Solomon reaped the benefit of his father David's godly life. Yet we must recognize that he also experienced the consequences of David's most glaring sins. Solomon's failures centered largely on his addiction to sexual sins. He married seven hundred women and had three hundred additional concubines to satisfy his sexual appetite. As he grew older, these women—many of them pagan idol worshippers—influenced Solomon to follow their practices. They were his downfall. As the chronicler of 1 Kings noted, "Solomon did evil in the eyes of the LORD; he did not follow the LORD completely, as David his father had done.... The LORD became angry with Solomon because his heart had turned away from the LORD, the God of Israel, who had appeared to him twice. Although he had forbidden Solomon to follow other gods, Solomon did not keep the LORD's command" (11:6, 9–10).

Solomon's sins were a direct result of his father, David's, darkest failures. The delayed-harvest principle was at work.

The effects of the father's sins were inescapable. And the tragedy of moral failure and idol worship didn't stop with Solomon. The descendants of this brilliant king, as well as the entire nation of Israel, shared in the delayed harvest of Solomon's wicked practices. Both Israel and Judah eventually fell into captivity as a judgment of their idolatrous ways. When there is no true repentance, the delayed harvest may seem to remain dormant for generations. But harvest time eventually rolls around on the calendar of God's justice.

Ted's footprints in the carpet point the way for parents who wish to march victoriously through fields full of weeds and dangerous enemies and produce for their children a good harvest.

2

The Principle of
Generational Transfer

I mentioned earlier that I carry a copy of an obituary in my briefcase. It recounts the life and legacy of my great-grandfather, "William Ludwig Bubeck. Born in Germany in 1830, born anew into God's family shortly after arriving in America in 1852. He lived eighty-five full years before God took him home early in the twentieth century."

Great-grandpa Bubeck's obituary clearly communicates his Christian testimony. Two other sentences of his life summary capture the tone of his Christian character: "He loved Christian people of all denominations, and his great soul looked upon the whole world as his Master's kingdom. He rejoiced in every movement that had for its object the establishment of that kingdom among men."

He was a man of prayer. My family continues to reap a harvest of blessing because of the seeds he sowed many years ago. I regularly read that obituary to remind myself of the blessings his life set in motion, which the Bubeck family still enjoys today.

From Grandparent to Parent to Child

Minta wasn't that fortunate. She came to my attention when her therapist sent her to me for counsel and evaluation. Though raised in a Jewish home, her parents were, for the most part, nonobservant Jews. Minta remembers her father as a hardworking materialist who "didn't know how to show love to any of his children." She saw him as critical, bitter, and miserable. He was murdered during a robbery attempt, and Minta recalled her feelings about his brutal death. "I felt guilty that I still hated him so much. He was never a part of my life when I needed him."

Her relationship with her mother was equally as painful. In Minta's written evaluation of her mother, she used words like manipulative, accusing, hateful, and complaining. Minta's mother also introduced her to fortune-telling, palm reading, and other occult practices.

Even after Minta became a follower of Christ she lacked joy. She battled many of the same character flaws that long plagued her family. She also experienced strange phenomena. "I see faces, shadows, and movements all of the time when I'm alone. I have regular visits from a spirit called Mike. He tells me what to do when I'm feeling bad." Her occult exposure through her mother had opened Minta to demonic harassment.

Generations of unbelief, occultism, rejection, and bitterness had left deep scars in Minta's life. Her own words reveal the generational origins of her struggles.

"I can see this generational thing so clearly. My dad was a heartless materialist just like my grandpa. I doubt if my dad ever heard a kind word of encouragement. He treated me just like he was treated. Mom carried on the same superstitious interests that her mother followed.

"My brothers and sisters are almost as messed up as I am. I can see in all of us the same loneliness, misery, and destructive behavior our parents and grandparents lived out."

As Minta thought about her family, tears born of insight flowed. "Oh, this has got to stop! I can already see my kids struggling with some of the same feelings and low self-esteem that plagued me all my life. It's affected our whole family."

The behavior of one generation sometimes seems to create a rut from which it is difficult for successive generations to escape.

A look at another family tells a different story.

Among the Rangels, three men in successive generations have been gifted pastors, yet each has engaged in adultery. Three generations of moral sin disgraced those men, their families, and their Lord's reputation. The harm they inflicted on their partners in sin has been equally disastrous.

How do we explain the passing of sinful tendencies from one generation to the next? Some people might suggest a genetic link. I still remember hearing my parents talk of strong character coming from "good stock" and weak character from "bad stock." But is genetics the best explanation for what went wrong with the Rangels? Hardly. The explanation has more to do with the spiritual realm than with environmental factors or human genetics.

A BETTER EXPLANATION

The phenomenon of "generational transfer" offers insight into persistent temptation and defeat. The Bible has a lot to say about generational transfer.

Positive and negative character traits seem to pass from generation to generation. Timothy M. Warner, of Trinity Evangelical Divinity School, addressed this important issue in his book, *Spiritual Warfare*.[1]

> One generation lives with the effects of the good or
> the bad done by the previous generation. That this

has application at the personal level is readily
accepted in the physical realm.... The same principle
applies in the spiritual area. Demons claim that if a
parent was giving them ground through unconfessed
sin in his or her life, they have the right to harass the
offspring of that person.... Renunciation of the sins
of parents and ancestors should be a standard part of
the conversion/discipleship process.

It is likely that we pass from generation to generation
both blessings and curses. The sinful failures of our forefathers yield consequences that can affect us today. To
understand this more fully, we need to go back to the
beginning.

ORIGINAL SIN AND GOD'S GRACE

The palms of my hands were sweaty. I paced about with
nervous tension. Thoughts raced through my mind: *Am I
prepared enough? Is the subject too heavy for my congregation? Do
I really understand the subject matter? Will I bore the people with
heavy teaching?* My leaders joined me in prayer. I went
before my congregation still tense but resolved to do my
best.

I remember those first experiences of preaching from
the book of Romans. It's one thing to learn about original
sin and its consequences in Bible college; it's quite another
to teach those principles to a hungry congregation. That's
particularly true when it comes to deep subjects like original sin and redemption. I used to wonder whether people
would benefit from my efforts. Would they understand
truth? But over time, thanks to the help of God and other
godly teachers, my people began to grasp the profound
truths of original sin and God's redemptive grace. Romans
5 highlights those key principles.

> Sin entered the world through one man, and death
> through sin, and in this way death came to all men,
> because all sinned.... But the gift is not like the tres-
> pass. For if the many died by the trespass of the one
> man, how much more did God's grace and the gift
> that came by the grace of the one man, Jesus Christ,
> overflow to the many! (vv. 12, 15)

Those verses encapsulate the message of the whole
Bible. It's an astonishing declaration with two main
thoughts. The first part of Paul's teaching is that sin and
death "entered" the story of the human race as the result
one man's disobedience. Guilt, condemnation, sin, and
death itself came upon humanity through the sinful disobedience of the first Adam. This is, in its most basic form,
generational transfer. Adam's sin brought the sentence of
death to every human being. His guilt became our guilt.

The second part of Paul's declaration is even more astonishing. Deliverance from spiritual death and the judgment we
deserve depends on the actions of one man. Jesus Christ
removes believers from the realm of guilt, sin, and death.
They actually enter a new realm of righteousness, joy, peace,
and everlasting life. All this is due to the person and work of
Jesus Christ alone. Salvation comes through Christ's work,
and nothing can separate us from what Christ has done. God
credits to every believer the merit and righteousness of
Christ. That transfer ensures our justification. He actually sees
us the way He sees His own Son.

How truly awesome is that? It will be the theme of our
worship throughout eternity. Revelation 5:9–10 eloquently
expresses that profound truth. "And they sang a new song:
'You are worthy to take the scroll and to open its seals,
because you were slain, and with your blood you purchased
men for God from every tribe and language and people and

nation. You have made them to be a kingdom and priests to serve our God, and they will reign on the earth.'"

Christ's magnificent work to redeem lost people will motivate angel choirs to sing, "Worthy is the Lamb, who was slain, to receive power and wealth and wisdom and strength and honor and glory and praise!" (Rev. 5:12). Adam's act condemned us all and established humanity's need of salvation. All our sinful desires have as their source the sinful nature we inherited from him. Likewise, our forgiveness required the transfer of another's merit to our own. The message of redeeming grace rests on the obedience of the sinless Son of God, Jesus Christ, and His atoning death. God transfers Christ's righteousness to us as if it were our own righteousness.

Saving grace grants equal benefits to every person who believes. Each receives eternal life. Every believer experiences a new birth, justification, forgiveness of sins, peace with God, citizenship in heaven, the indwelling of the Holy Spirit, and membership in the body of Christ. These benefits come to us at the moment we trust Jesus Christ for salvation. His life, His worthiness, His riches, His righteousness, and His standing before God extend in equal measure to all who receive Him as Lord and Savior.

TRANSFER OF OUR FATHER'S SINS

The consequences of Adam's original sin transferred to every subsequent member of the human race. Each of us became equally guilty, equally lost, equally helpless, and equally in need of saving grace. But there is a second kind of transfer that is *unequal* in its application.

Whereas Adam's sin transferred equally to us its consequences, the effects of our own family issues vary widely. Their consequences are sometimes subtle, but they are no less the fulfillment of God's warning that He would afflict "the iniquity of the fathers upon the children and the children's children to the third and fourth generation" (Ex. 34:7 NKJV).

WHAT GENERATIONAL TRANSFER *DOESN'T* MEAN

I have heard counselees tell me, "My sufferings and sin problems are all due to the sins and failures of my ancestors." Be careful. We cannot cite our parents' sins as excuses for our own. Generational transfer does not mean our sins are our parents' responsibility.

We have no right to blame our ancestors for our sinful choices. My friend Jim suffered from such a passive and fatalistic view of his struggles. He saw himself as a victim of his genes and family environment. His personal breakthrough happened only after he realized redeeming grace, biblical truth, and the work of the Holy Spirit could free him from the disastrous patterns he followed.

The prophet Ezekiel declared God's rebuke for such faulty thinking:

> What do you people mean by quoting this proverb about the land of Israel: "The fathers eat sour grapes, and the children's teeth are set on edge"? As surely as I live, declares the Sovereign LORD, you will no longer quote this proverb in Israel. For every living soul belongs to me, the father as well as the son— both alike belong to me. The soul who sins is the one who will die. (Ezek. 18:2–4)

Ezekiel's point? It was wrong to blame "the fathers" for the judgment God was administering. It is equally invalid today to blame one's parents for a personal attraction to sin. The words of the prophets echo an excuse I still hear today: "I can't help sinning in these ways because I inherited the tendency from my father."

Bible commentator G. Campbell Morgan put it this way:

> If your teeth are on edge, do not blame your father.
> Whosoever eateth sour grapes, his teeth shall be set
> on edge. If your teeth are on edge, you have eaten
> the sour grapes.
>
> "Yes, but my father did eat them, and I had a ten-
> dency to sour grapes before I was born." Is that so?
> Then God is greater than your father, and the forces
> that He places at your disposal are greater than all
> your tendency toward sour grapes.
>
> "Yes, but I have eaten them myself. I plead guilty.
> God help me, I am guilty. I have eaten them. My
> teeth are on edge, and I have contracted a liking for
> sour grapes! Though I hate them, I must have them."
>
> God is greater than one's liking. Get back to Him. He
> will put Himself between you and your father and
> between you and your past, for the river of God is
> flowing, and there is life wherever the river comes.[2]

There is a relationship between the sins of a father and those of a son, but the personal accountability of each individual supersedes the transfer. "Every living soul belongs to me," God says (Ezek. 18:4). The father and the son are equally accountable to God for their own sins.

WHAT GENERATIONAL TRANSFER *DOES* MEAN

Believers must try to understand how God visits the sins of the fathers on the children to the third and fourth generations. Several factors require careful thought.

First, *a parent's sinful choices of environment and example will have far-reaching consequences on his or her children and grandchildren.* Many correctly see the basic message of God's warning as a reference to the influences of the home environment. As children suffer the consequences of their parents' influence, they tend to pass those negatives to the next generation. It certainly makes sense. Children who grow up in a climate of profanity, pornography, substance abuse, and immorality become victims. Dysfunctional parents create dysfunctional families. The adult children of such families tend to perpetuate the same patterns. They may hate the old patterns but feel just as helpless to escape their snare.

Second, *a parent's abusive behavior often yields long-term consequences for the children.* Recall from chapter 1 how Linn described her godly father's footprints in the carpet. When Ted entered his children's rooms to pray over them as they slept, there were benefits they received later in life. Linn still fondly remembers those visits, and her life continues today to have as her guiding principle the desire to please God. It was a pattern her father helped to establish.

Tragically, however, the nightly visits of some fathers are not so noble. We often hear of quiet nighttime visits from a dad who, instead of praying, *preys* sexually on his daughter or son. Other fathers verbally assault their children, using words to cut, belittle, and reject their kids. Many go so far as to physically batter their children in fits of rage.

The wounds of abuse can last a lifetime. Healing is a long and difficult road. But of all the forms of abuse, few have more devastating consequences than sexual abuse. It rips apart a child's self-esteem, security, and trust. The only activity more damaging is parent-sponsored satanic ritual abuse.

These issues frequently transfer from one generation to another. A sexually abusive parent was often himself the victim of sexual abuse. Abusers tend to produce abusers.

Dave experienced such a transfer. He came to me for counseling because of the violent outbursts of anger he was experiencing toward his own children. Dave loved them deeply. It tormented him to see the fear in his children's eyes when they thought they had offended him. As we processed, he finally admitted that at times he felt strong sexual urges toward his son. He couldn't understand how a Christian father would have such a perverse attraction toward his own son.

He had successfully to this point resisted that temptation, but the very thought gnawed at him. As Dave spoke openly about it, he was able to recognize that God understood and wanted to help him find freedom. Over time and through prayer, Dave eventually recalled events he had long ago forgotten. Both his father and grandfather had sexually violated him. But Dave had repressed every conscious memory of those crimes.

The recovery of his memories was crucial to his own healing, but new spiritual and psychological struggles began to emerge. He had to forgive both a dead grandfather and a living father. It would require much grace and wisdom from God.

Dave worked hard. God graciously enabled him to confront and to forgive his aging father. It was an experience of healing for both of them. Dave's anger toward his son lessened, and he was able to resist the sexual temptations. The grace of our Lord Jesus Christ heals the sins of the fathers even when the wounds are deep and painful.

Third, *a parent's sinful physical vices produce negative consequences on children.* Health professionals universally acknowledge the havoc the sins of the parents can wreak in their children. The difference is that they don't call it sin; they simply call it inappropriate behavior. Whatever the terminology, the outcomes are the same: Little babies enter the world addicted to crack; they suffer the effects of fetal alcohol syndrome; they register a low birth weight because of exposure to nicotine-laden smoke. Just ask the adult child of an alcoholic who, even though he despises his alcoholic parent, can't seem to let go of the bottle. Then there is the child born HIV-positive or with some other sexually transmitted disease with which his parent infected him. The sins of our parents carry profound consequences that last a lifetime.

HOW TO LIMIT THE TRANSFERENCE OF SIN'S CONSEQUENCES

We overcome negative generational transference with consistent prayers and godly examples. Conversely, the neglect of prayer and godly living on the part of a parent renders our children more vulnerable to transference.

The desire to leave a positive legacy should strengthen our determination not to pass our sins to the next generation. We must recognize the great benefit our godly example can be to those who follow behind us. Timothy, the young pastor who Paul addressed in two of his letters, wasn't the only son and grandson to benefit from a godly mother and grandmother. (See 2 Tim. 1:5.)

Some of us, however, have no alternative but to face life without the supportive prayers of godly ancestors. This places us at a disadvantage. I, myself, am thankful to be the recipient of a godly heritage. But for those who find themselves in a different place, it's essential to rely on the love and grace of God that are able to overrule the spiritual and emotional deficits of an unfortunate upbringing.

THE INFLUENCE OF ANCESTORS VICTIMIZED BY THE ADVERSARY

Generational transfer of sin can come from another source: demonized ancestors—people who demons have either inhabited or influenced. The activity and influence of demons are factors in the transference of sin and its consequences onto our children. Demons work hard to transfer the fruit of their "ministry" from one generation to the next.

We must, of course, be careful not to imply that the sinful patterns in children always indicate demonic activity. Each of us can sin with the worst of humanity without any need for a nudge from the kingdom of darkness. "The heart is deceitful above all things, and desperately wicked; who can know it?" (Jer. 17:9 NKJV). Our bent toward sin needs little encouragement.

And demons love to harass little children. Jesus confronted a challenge with a demonized boy when He came down the mountain after His transfiguration (Matt. 17:14–23; Mark 9:17–29; Luke 9:37–42). Mark's gospel account confirms that the demonization had been a part of the son's life from "childhood, referring to someone under seven years old." The problem became apparent early in the child's life, well before he could have willfully chosen to open his life to demonic powers through immorality or idolatry.

It is unlikely that any personal sin on the boy's part led to his demonic harassment. But if the boy's possession by the demon was not the result of his own actions, what was the cause? The explanation is similar to the cause of other maladies that plague our children. It was due to the sins of the previous generations. This kind of transference happens all the time. Drug-addicted babies didn't become addicts by their own wrongdoing. The mother physically transferred her addiction to the unborn child.

The issues we pass to the next generation go beyond the physical and psychological. We also transfer spiritual consequences to our children. This is how this demonized little boy's problems began. He was a victim of generational wickedness. A previous family member had somewhere along the line opened a door to demonic forces. It could have been a parent, grandparent, or even an aunt or uncle who did so. And it produced a tragic consequence.

This particular demon's strength and authority must have been immense. The disciples couldn't deal with it. Jesus indicated in this case the need for prayer and even fasting to overcome the power of such an evil spirit. How did such a powerful demon stake a claim on that young boy?

It could be that a family member from a previous generation had involved himself in occult practices. Involvement in the occult can open any person's life to demonic activity and control. The Bible warns us of the terrible consequences of involvement in the occult. "The sacrifices of pagans are offered to demons, not to God, and I do not want you to be participants with demons. You cannot drink the cup of the Lord and the cup of demons too; you cannot have a part in both the Lord's table and the table of demons" (1 Cor. 10:20–21).

The deeper a person delves into spiritistic (communication with the dead or with spirits) activities, the more he opens his life to demonic forces. This young child may well have had previous family members who participated in idol worship, which was common in those days. Idol worship is really demon worship. Perhaps the relative had died, but demons never die. They will harass generation after generation to destroy people who bear the image of God.

The issue of generational transfer is an important aspect of God's dealings with individuals and even entire cultures. When God spared Nineveh, one of the reasons He offered was, "Nineveh has more than a hundred and twenty thousand people who cannot tell their right hand from their left.... Should I not be concerned about that great city?" (Jonah 4:11).

He was probably referring in that verse to the children who lived in Nineveh. The Lord confronted Jonah for his callous lack of concern for the children of that city. God's concern for the little ones of Nineveh is nice, but how do we explain God's decisions to wipe out entire cultures, including children?

God's promises to Abraham shed some light on the problem. The Lord had promised to give the land in which the Canaanites were living to Abraham and his offspring. But that promise wouldn't find fulfillment for a long time. Abraham didn't have a son for many years after God made the promise. Then God tells Abraham in Genesis 15 about the four-hundred-year captivity of his descendants in Egypt. His explanation to Abraham is profound: "In the fourth generation your descendants will come back here, for the sin of the Amorites has not yet reached its full measure" (v. 16).

The destruction of Canaanite culture would not take place until their sins were "full." Only then would God command Joshua and his armies to destroy every man, woman, and child. But why kill the children, too? It was due to the demonization of the entire culture. The worship of false gods (which are really demons) and total moral degeneracy had filled their cup to overflowing. The Canaanite-Amorite culture was beyond repair and had exhausted God's patience and mercy. The generational wickedness had demonized the whole culture. It required the destruction of every person; otherwise, the generational transfer of wickedness would have continued, generation after generation.

Ed Murphy, in his book on spiritual warfare, listed six sin areas that lead to the demonization of believers. The first has to do with generational sin.[3] C. Fred Dickason, an expert on the occult, claimed that 95 percent of the cases of demonization he has seen "are due to an ancestor's involvement in occult and demonic activities."[4]

Demonic activity tends to follow generational lines. A majority of the troubled people I've been able to help have a family history of occult involvement. Where, then, can we find hope? We find it, above all else, in the salvation available through the Lord Jesus Christ. That salvation is able to disrupt the schemes of the Adversary and to prevent the transfer of demonic control from generation to generation.

COMING FREE

The redeeming power of our Lord Jesus Christ is able to set free any person from the consequences of generational sin. In Christ, we are already more than conquerors because we are one with Him and He has already conquered the forces of darkness.

But we must never be smug about our victory. Our walk of faith requires an aggressive application of our freedom. This includes the generational transference of sin that threatens to harm the next generation. Christ's finished work is able to protect and free us and our children from the transfer of the harmful aspects of a delayed harvest. We need to *know* it, to *pray* it, and to *live* it by faith.

The apostle Peter had deep compassion for the hurting believers who were under attack by the world system in which they lived, as well as the Devil and his kingdom. He likely had the generational transfer issue in mind when the Holy Spirit inspired these words: "Since you call on a Father who judges each man's work impartially, live your lives as strangers here in reverent fear. For you know that it was not with perishable things such as silver or gold that you were redeemed from the empty way of life *handed down to you from your forefathers*, but with the precious blood of Christ, a lamb without blemish or defect" (1 Peter 1:17–19).

The blood of Christ removes the necessity of a delayed harvest that is due to our forefathers' sinful practices. Yet we must not passively assume our protection. Truth without action is a dangerous presumption. We must obediently stand in the absolutes of God's truth as we face all our enemies. It is an obedient response to truth that sets us free from the rule of all that opposes God's will.

The power of prayer to defeat the Adversary is available. In my book *Overcoming the Adversary*, I told the story of one woman who had seizures while she slept. Her medical diagnosis was "anxiety attacks." But they involved something much deeper and darker.

We discussed the possibility of Satan's involvement. Not only were the seizures painful, but they were frightening as well. We carefully considered our biblical authority as believers to refuse Satan the right to rule any area of our lives. In Romans 6 this woman saw her privilege and responsibility to "not let sin reign in your mortal body so that you obey its evil desires" (v. 12).

A careful procedure was planned. We talked of how the husband could come to his wife's rescue by challenging any spirit of darkness behind the seizure. The next time a seizure began, the woman and her husband were immediately to challenge any of Satan's involvement by forbidding him to rule in this way. He was to say,

> *In the name of the Lord Jesus Christ and by the power of His blood, I resist any spirit of darkness that is trying to cause my wife to have a seizure. I forbid you to do it. I command you to leave our presence and to go where the Lord Jesus Christ sends you.*

He was urged to insist repeatedly until the seizure was broken. His wife was encouraged as best she was able to repeat the challenge her husband addressed against Satan.

As our friends utilized this strategy, the seizures ceased completely. In this case demons had indeed been involved and were seeking to intensify a human weakness.[5] The process of stepping into freedom may require years to complete. The powers behind the initial attack against the woman I mentioned above went down in defeat and departed. She gladly served the Lord in a variety of roles and was an exemplary wife and mother.

Part of the process in overcoming our heritage lies in learning to pray prevailing prayers, which paralyze our Adversary and loosen the hold he has on our lives. We find in Christ ultimate freedom. A delayed harvest of darkness, when we bring it to Christ, can be turned to glory.

**SPECIFIC, PREVAILING
PRAYERS ARE AN
IMPORTANT COMPONENT
IN OVERCOMING
THE ADVERSARY IN
OUR HOMES.**

3

Prayers That Paralyze the Adversary

CLARISSA'S STORY

The Brandons, a mature Christian couple, had adopted Clarissa when she was just three days old. Clarissa was the recipient of tender loving care, discipline, and educational opportunities. She also participated weekly in a strong Bible-believing church. Despite these opportunities, Clarissa became increasingly difficult to handle. Rebellion, cursing, violent actions, and bizarre behavior patterns caused her parents to seek professional help. The psychiatrist and social workers finally conceded defeat and recommended that the Brandons institutionalize Clarissa.

Clarissa's behavior worsened until, at the age of ten, she was too dangerous for her parents to handle. Her acts of violence made school attendance impossible. Her parents had prayed often throughout this ordeal. They read my books on spiritual warfare and called me for counsel. I suggested that they investigate the history of her biological family. Finally the Brandons brought Clarissa to see me. Since she was uncooperative, my counseling focused on her parents.

They told me what they had learned from their study of

Clarissa's biological lineage. Both parents had been involved in a lifestyle that included prostitution, witchcraft, drug abuse, and alcoholism. It struck me that at least part of Clarissa's struggle might be due to sin that we could trace back over multiple generations.

The parents began to pray aggressively on behalf of their adopted daughter. I instructed them to claim their spiritual position as the rightful protective parental authority over Clarissa. They firmly resisted in prayer the powers of darkness that, because of the sinful practices of her biological parents, were controlling Clarissa. They asked the Lord Jesus Christ to sever any bloodline claims the Adversary might exercise against their daughter. Whenever they witnessed behavior that suggested attempts by the Adversary to rule Clarissa, they practiced this kind of prevailing prayer.

As the Brandons claimed their spiritual position of authority and oversight over Clarissa, they began to see remarkable, positive change in their daughter. Her caseworkers could not believe the difference.

The response of these parents reminds us that specific, prevailing prayers are an important component in overcoming the Adversary in our homes. Such prayers will diminish and even eliminate the effects of a delayed harvest in our lives.

SUZY'S STORY

Mary and Jim sought my counsel because their five-year-old daughter, Suzy, regularly lost control of herself in violent rages. The problem became so severe that on one occasion Mary called her husband at his office. She was terrified.

"Jim, you must come home immediately," Mary pleaded. "I'm afraid of our daughter."

Suzy had displayed abnormal strength, overpowering her mother, even though she was only five years old. She would regularly curse and make violent threats against her parents. All attempts to discipline her during these episodes were in vain.

I asked Jim and Mary during my first session with them if anyone on either side of their family lineage had shown similar, out-of-control anger rages. There was the possibility of a generational delayed harvest. Jim and Mary looked at each other and smiled. Though reared in a religious home, Jim had come to faith in Christ as an adult. His father had repeatedly battered Jim during numerous out-of-control rages. Jim was now as a believer trying to gain release from bitterness and to forgive his father for his abuse.

I discussed with Jim and Mary the principle of sowing and reaping and the delayed harvest and then suggested a simple plan to help Suzy. The next time Suzy began her out-of-control behavior, Jim would respond by gently gathering her into his arms. He would restrain her flailing arms, scratching fingers, and kicking legs and pray aloud the following prayer:

Heavenly Father, in the name of my Lord Jesus Christ and by the power of His blood, I renounce any generational rage that is seeking to control Suzy. I forbid all such control and ask the Holy Spirit to calm and control Suzy by His loving presence and to take control of her mind, will, emotions, and body.

Jim followed those instructions the next time Suzy "lost it." She had become violent, exhibiting great strength, screaming, cursing, and biting. But as Jim began to pray, he felt her relax. In the midst of his prayer, she turned her face to his, kissed him on the cheek, and tenderly said, "I love you, Daddy!"

This marked a turning point in Suzy's life. Her parents continue to protect her by their prayers and to teach her how to overcome her anger in a biblical way. Suzy is now maturing into a beautiful and godly young lady.

MISCONCEPTIONS ABOUT GOD AND THE DELAYED HARVEST

There are three common misconceptions about the legacy of our parents' sins that we must correct.

MISCONCEPTION 1: THERE IS NO ESCAPE

Some people assume they are doomed to failure because of the sins of previous generations. They may think, *My mother was a drug addict, and my addiction is consistent with the family tradition.* Or, *My dad was an alcoholic, so I guess I'm destined to be one too.*

Defeatist attitudes and pangs of guilt plague many of us because we feel bound by the unhealthy past of our families. But God's grace not only saves us, it has the power to redeem dysfunctional patterns. That's not to imply that a relationship with Christ immediately solves all our problems. Emotional healing often requires considerable time, nurture, and loving counsel. But the starting point is a real relationship with God through Jesus Christ. The first step for any person who seeks to overcome a negative family history is to be sure of your salvation and to recognize that your ultimate freedom rests on the resurrection power of Jesus Christ who now lives in you.

I once spoke at a spiritual warfare conference in a small Minnesota town. It was there that I met Jessica. She sat in the second row with her husband, Fred. Jessica's face wore a mask of gloom and despair. Her body language shouted, "I'm hopeless." I found her expression so distracting that I purposely avoided eye contact with her.

The pastor invited any conference attendee needing help to arrange an appointment with me. The first request for help was from Jessica.

Jessica informed me that she came from a dysfunctional family. She described her abusive parents as alcoholics and "drug heads." Anger, bitterness, and a sense of inescapable failure ruled Jessica's heart. She was at the point of utter despair.

I asked Jessica to share with me her salvation experience. She claimed to be a "good" person who had always done everything at the church without anyone needing to ask. She was faithful to every service. That was the extent of her personal story. Trusting Christ for salvation was not part of it. I knew where we needed to start.

Jessica needed to understand God's grace. We spent the next hour looking into the Word of God about salvation. The Holy Spirit worked in her heart, and she invited the Lord Jesus Christ into her life to save her from her sins and her lost condition. She asked God to remove all the hurt, anger, and harm from her dysfunctional background. I led her in a renunciation of any claim the Adversary was using against her because of her own sins or those of her prior generations.

The change was dramatic. When the pastor and his wife saw Jessica they exclaimed, "What happened to you, Jessica?" She was radiant. The joy of the Lord seemed to burst forth from her. Like the woman at the well in John 4, Jessica's cup was full and running over.

Everyone at the next session of the conference also noticed. People kept saying, "It's obvious something good has happened in your life." She told them that Jesus Christ had set her free from sin and death. Her message was compelling. The darkness was gone; in its place was peace and light.

The message is simple. The saving grace of Christ is sufficient to free all who come to Him. The hurts and harms of our dysfunctional past fall in defeat before His grace.

Many people go through the motions of baptism, church membership, and church life without ever having experienced a spiritual new birth. In the absence of true salvation, the darkness of Jessica's past persisted. Cleansing and healing grace were beyond her reach until she reached the point of surrender, which is where all real healing begins. A person must enter a real relationship with God through Christ before the resources to combat generational sin become available.

MISCONCEPTION 2: GOD IS PUNISHING ME

Bill, a friend of mine from high school, carried throughout his life feelings of false guilt and unworthiness. Bill's father was a convicted felon. The arrest, trial, and conviction brought to his family both poverty and shame. Bill's father eventually committed suicide, which only added to the burden his son carried. The insensitive comments of others compounded his sense that God was punishing him for his father's offense. All my encouragement of Bill seemed to have no effect.

After high school we drifted apart. I finally heard one day some distressing news. Bill, like his father, had taken his own life. He had performed the ultimate self-punishment for his father's wrongdoings.

Bill was a victim of the Adversary's deception. God doesn't expect us to atone for our fathers' sins. Deuteronomy 24:16 establishes this principle: "Fathers shall not be put to death for their children, nor children put to death for their fathers; each is to die for his own sin."

God's justice does not permit human courts to assign ancestral guilt to children. If children have not participated in the crime a parent or grandparent has committed, they deserve no punishment. Personal guilt before God depends on our own individual records. Judgment and eternal wrath fall on us, not because of what Mom and Dad have done; they are the results of *our own* transgressions of God's laws. Condemnation awaits only those who fail to appropriate the mercy and forgiveness available through the blood of Christ. Each person dies for his own sin, not the sins of his forebears. Likewise, a parent's salvation doesn't automatically transfer to a son or daughter. Each one of us, regardless of how godly our parents may have been, must personally receive salvation through Jesus Christ. God holds each of us personally and individually accountable.

But there is something else to consider: Even though God safeguards children from legal guilt for their parents' sins, it is possible for our kids to suffer some nasty consequences as a result of Mom's or Dad's transgressions. The damage can wreak havoc over multiple generations. Take, for example, the flood of Noah's day, the destruction of Sodom and Gomorrah, the fall of Jericho, and the annihilation of the entire Canaanite culture. Infants, children, and even animals suffered God's judgment. We will focus later on why God's judgment occurs in such instances. At this point, however, we must stress the norm in God's dealings with *His own people*. The bottom line is this: An ancestor's wickedness will neither keep one from salvation nor will it make spiritual victory impossible in a Christian's life.

MISCONCEPTION 3: GOD IS UNFAIR

It seems unfair to many people that God would allow the consequences of our parents' behavior to negatively impact subsequent generations. It just *feels* wrong. But in our discomfort with God's judgments, we generally fail to recognize our inability to see things from His perspective. Our human limitations render us incapable of understanding even a tiny portion of God's sovereign actions. There is much about God's plans that we simply don't understand—yet.

God's ways are always just and holy. Justice, truth, and holiness are attributes of His nature and character. Justice is part of the very essence of His being, and our questions are merely symptoms of our inability to see life, time, and eternity from His vantage point. (See Job 38—42.)

We prove our ignorance when we tell God how to work out His justice. It is legitimate to express our questions to God, but we must do so with the recognition that His ways are much higher than ours. Our prayer should be,

> *Lord, I don't see how this fits into Your love and mercy, but I want to. I know Your ways are always holy, just, and loving. You could not be anything else.*

God can help those who are experiencing the negative outcomes of a delayed harvest; He responds to the prayers of His people. We have a God who bestows His grace on unworthy humans. That's important to know in this twenty-first century where drug use, sexual obsession, and devotion to the occult are common. With evil all around us, we need to use our spiritual resources to walk wisely in spiritual freedom—and to help our children find that freedom.

We must, therefore, understand and become practitioners of God's truth. We will then be able to help families gain freedom from the ravages of the delayed harvest.

PREVAILING PRAYER

We began this book with the story of Linn, who recalled her father's "footprints in the carpet" as he prayed for her every night. Let's take a closer look at Ted and his wife, Chris, to see how parents can protect their children from the Adversary in their home. Their story reveals how parents and their children can be free from the unfortunate effects of the delayed harvest.

Early in their marriage Ted and Chris came to our church. They had been believers for only a few years and found at our church the spiritual nurture they needed. We quickly became good friends.

God began to lead Ted and Chris into a deeper understanding of faith and prayer. They had tried for six years to conceive but without success. It was in this crisis that Ted began to learn about faith and prayer. "I was sitting in church with the congregation," Ted said, "and I remember committing to the Lord the children that I believed God was going to give us. I told the Lord I would dedicate them to Him and trust Him with their future. I promised the Lord that Chris and I would do our utmost to give them the spiritual guidance and direction that they would need to grow to love and serve the Lord."

As Ted finished his prayer the peace of God settled on him. God eventually blessed this couple with a daughter, Linn. Three years later, Peter was born. From the moment they became aware of each pregnancy, these parents began to pray for that child. After the birth of both children, Ted and Chris continued to pray daily over Linn and Peter, especially at bedtime.

Ted and I once attended a weeklong evangelism conference. Ted heard me pray for our families each day the prevailing, spiritual-warfare-style of prayer that had become my practice. Ted would later tell me, "It was there I learned to use my authority to pray against the influence of Satan and his kingdom. It started a revolution in my prayer life, especially as it related to how I prayed for my children."

When Ted returned home, he established the habit that left his footprints in the carpet. Each night after the children were sleeping, Ted entered each child's room and prayed a prevailing spiritual-warfare prayer over them. They would occasionally awaken to hear Dad praying quietly. As they grew older, they would occasionally tease Dad about his "long, boring prayers." But they learned to appreciate the value of those nightly intercessions. Peter and Linn were recently home from college for a long weekend. It was then that Linn approached her mother and tearfully asked, "Is Dad still going in our rooms each night to pray for us even though we are away at college?"

Ted's prayers, as he learned to utilize his position in Christ and to intercede, made a difference in his daughter's life. His action serves as a model of how we as parents can pass to our children a delayed harvest of blessings.

I asked Ted to share with me one of his "footprints in the carpet" prayers. Ted recorded a prayer for me, and now I share it with you. May the Lord raise up a multitude of dads willing to pray for their children like Ted does for his.

> *Our great God and heavenly Father, I humbly come before You in the name of the Lord Jesus Christ. By the power of His shed blood, I claim Christ's victory over sin, Satan, and all his principalities and powers of darkness. I ask that Satan and all his evil powers assigned against my family would be bound and rendered unable to work their wicked plans against Linn, Peter, Chris, or me. I position my family under the protective blood of my Lord Jesus Christ, and I claim all the promises You have given to us through Your Son. I claim the promise of eternal life, of salvation, and of life with You in Your eternal kingdom.*
>
> *Dear God and Father of our Lord Jesus Christ, I worship You and give You thanks for all that You have done in our lives. Thank You that we can approach the great and powerful God of Abraham, Isaac, and Jacob. Thank You for the cross of Calvary, for the sacrifice of Your Son who died that we might live and have eternal life with You. In the name of*

the Lord Jesus Christ, I ask that any strongholds Satan's kingdom has established in our lives would be torn down and destroyed. I ask You to forbid Satan or any of his demons from having any effect on Linn, Peter, Chris, or me.

Heavenly Father, station the holy angels round about us to protect us and to keep us safe from the evil and harm that might be near. I pray that Your Holy Spirit will fully control our hearts and our lives to remind us of our kinship and sonship with You. Please focus our attention on You. Guide us with Your eye that we would be conscious of who we are—a part of Your family who forever follows after You.

I pray specifically for Linn. Minister to her in a special way today. Keep Your holy hand on her. Grant her strength, wisdom, power, and sharpness of mind. Grant her a spiritual hunger to seek after You. I pray, heavenly Father, for You to raise up a Christian young man who loves the Lord and would love Linn. Draw her to him and him to her at just the precise moment You have planned. May theirs be a happy Christian home all of their days.*

I pray the same for Peter. Raise up a Christian young woman whom he will deeply love and who will return his love with deep devotion as his helpmate. May You bless both of our children with their own children and grandchildren who will walk after God and serve You from the earliest days of their lives. Help Peter in all of his choices of life to always seek Your guidance and wisdom.

If it pleases Your will, Chris and I would like to enjoy our children's children before You call us home. I look to You to keep Your hand on our family in all of our ways. Protect us from the wiles of Satan, the *allure of the world, and the deceitfulness of sin. Please keep us surrounded with Your holy, protecting angels. Draw each one of us closer to You because we pray in the name of our Lord Jesus Christ with thanksgiving. Amen.*

*Linn has completed her college degree and has married a deeply committed Christian. God has blessed them with children, and they are seeking to guide them into God's ways of truth. Peter too completed college and has established a Christian home with the wife God provided him. The generational blessings are actively flowing on.

Part 2

SECURING OUR HOMES AGAINST THE ADVERSARY

4

Parents Who Love Each Other

Jennifer's eyes began to fill with tears the moment she took her seat. While she struggled for composure, I prayed for the Lord's peace and comfort. But as Jennifer tried to explain why she had come, her body trembled. Then, dabbing at her eyes, she poured out her story.

"I'm so ashamed. I'm finding it difficult to live with myself. I completely lost control of my anger. Rage and very nasty words poured out of me against Russ. I even threw a vase at him, and it broke into a million pieces. He was yelling at me, too! We were a first-class mess. What really breaks my heart is that Sammy and little Jenny saw all of this. They looked so lost and afraid."

Jennifer lapsed into uncontrolled sobbing. After she regained her composure, words of repentance poured out. "Oh, Lord! I'm so sorry! I'm so sorry! Please forgive me and please heal the hurt of our children! They're so little and we hurt them so much." A new rush of tears and sobs added poignancy to the moment.

Touched by her sincere brokenness, my own eyes

brimmed with tears. "Does Russ regret what happened as much as you do, Jennifer?" I asked. I knew quarrels sometimes leave lingering scars and resentments that can drive people apart. They may blame each other and reject their own personal responsibility.

Her reddened eyes quickly locked onto my gaze. "Oh yes! Russ feels as ashamed as I do. He can't believe how two people who love each other could be so angry and mean—especially when they're Christians!

"This doesn't happen often, but when it does we blow it, big time! We both saw how our anger frightened and crushed Sammy and Jenny, and we know something has to change. We really need help!"

I gave a sigh of relief. The desire to change in such cases is a prerequisite for any hope of recovery. I then addressed her fear.

"When you both know that, Jennifer, you've conquered a major hurdle," I assured her. "I'm so glad you came because I believe I can help you find that level of freedom the Lord has for you and Russ! You're wise to recognize the harm to your children, but God may well use it for good. The pain of your problem has served to motivate action. As you learn to walk in your freedom, you'll be able to teach your children to walk in theirs."

LOVE VERSUS FEAR

Children suffer deeply when their parents act harshly toward each other. Feelings of fear and guilt usually plague a child exposed to such behavior. A child often feels he is responsible for his parents' anger. He is unable to assign responsibility to them. The child's security, which finds its basis in his parents' love for each other, evaporates. Panic sets in.

The words of the apostle John have application to Christian parents. "There is no fear in love. But perfect love drives out fear, because fear has to do with punishment. The one who fears is not made perfect in love. We love because he first loved us" (1 John 4:18–19).

Failure to understand the damage that parental conflict places on our children's lives is dangerous. The flip side, of course, is that our kids enjoy great security when they see parents who deeply love and respect each other but can also in a biblical manner navigate serious conflict. God calls Christian parents to provide that kind of security for their children.

The most important way to love our children is to love our spouses. By doing so we establish a foundation that steadies our children against the attack of the Adversary. Consider John's warning in 1 John 4: "If anyone says, 'I love God,' yet hates his brother, he is a liar. For anyone who does not love his brother, whom he has seen, cannot love God, whom he has not seen. And he has given us this command: Whoever loves God must also love his brother" (vv. 20–21). These words are especially applicable to Christian couples.

To "love our brother" is a principle that finds application in marriage relationships. The capacity to control anger and to speak with love and respect to one's spouse is part of Christian grace. It goes hand in hand with faith. Our Christian walk meets its greatest test in the home. When it works there, everyone benefits from the security: our spouse, our children, and of course, ourselves. Even the neighbors will notice. And we will grow in intimacy with our spouses, as well as in the effectiveness of our parenting. To love our spouse is to protect our children.

THE POWER OF A STRONG MARRIAGE

Christians must provide a counterbalance to the destructive trends of contemporary culture. The well-being of our children depends on it. The Christian faith becomes real to children when they see its transforming power at work in their parents. The consistent modeling of spiritual values communicates powerfully to children. Showing love and forgiveness and putting others first are actions that strengthen our children's faith and enable them to face the future with confidence.

Children learn values by observing them in the people they know best. When they see parents applying biblical principles, those principles become more than a set of rules. They see living demonstrations of patience, forgiveness, kindness, and love, and they are likely to make those values their own.

Loving our spouse not only makes our Christian faith appealing to our children, but also influences our culture. Godliness has a long reach. Jesus tells us we are to be light that dispels darkness and to be salt that inhibits corruption. When the Holy Spirit controls a believer at the family level, it radiates into the world. The difference is strikingly apparent to those who bear the wounds a sinful culture inflicts.

In his classic book *How to Really Love Your Child*, Christian psychiatrist D. Ross Campbell emphasizes the love of husband and wife for each other as the prerequisite to effective parenting. The most important relationship in the family is the marital relationship. It takes primacy over all others, including the parent-child relationship. Both the quality of the parent-child bond and the child's security are largely dependent on the quality of the marital bond. So you can see why it is important to ensure the best possible relationship between wife and husband before seriously attempting to relate to your child in more positive ways.... The stronger and healthier this bond is, the fewer problems we will encounter as parents.[1]

When Mom and Dad demonstrate love for one another in

front of the children, it breeds security in their children. No other factor is as important. This kind of love needs to be our top priority. But it isn't easy. The struggle to make ends meet, along with the moral decline of our postmodern Western culture, tends to wear down our reserves. Only God's grace working in concert with our deep personal commitment will enable us to nurture a secure marital environment for our children.

Mary and Sid, both of them hardworking and successful, seemed to be deeply in love. But I knew their story: Married in their mid-twenties, well educated, and committed to loving each other, they encountered rocky places that could have devastated their marriage. Work tensions, several moves due to job changes, and strong personalities tested the durability of their love. They pursued counseling with me. The breakthrough came when one day I asked them to write down their biggest secret to surviving the trials they had suffered through as a married couple.

Here's what Sid wrote: "The demonstration of my parents' love commitment tested through the real-life encounters of their forty-plus years together is the single most influential element in my love for Mary. It's the cement that keeps my commitment glued in loving focus. Seeing that same commitment mirrored in the marriage of my wife's parents helps me know that we can and will make it. My commitment is fixed. It's the only option!"

Mary's written explanation echoed her husband's. She attributed her commitment to her parents' unconditional love for each other. "Their devotion to each other motivated my determination and prayer focus [on] parental love and security. I know it's God's plan. I refuse anything less for my girls. I keep looking to my Lord for the ability to love [Sid] with the forgiving encouragement and sensitive tenderness my parents showed and my Lord has for me."

OVERCOMING A PAINFUL PAST

Sid and Mary had parents who served as a model for them. But what if you didn't have loving parents to set an example? Maybe your home life was a disaster. Does that doom you to repeat the catastrophe? No! God's grace and mercy can overcome the worst of a dysfunctional heritage.

Josh McDowell, a prominent Christian author and conference speaker, is an exemplary husband and father. Yet his alcoholic father neglected him and even battered his mother. "Sometimes I'd go to the barn and find my mother lying [there] behind the cows, beaten so badly she couldn't get up. I hated my father for treating her so cruelly, and to avenge that treatment I would do everything I could to humiliate or punish him."[2]

The wounds of family dysfunction could have spelled permanent disaster for Josh, but God's grace and mercy were at work. After struggling with the credibility of the Christian faith, Josh finally trusted Jesus Christ as his Savior, an event that began a personal transformation. He would eventually meet Dick Day, who, despite his upbringing in a dysfunctional family, had built a loving marriage. Dick deeply loved his wife, Charlotte. As a result, Josh wrote, Dick and Charlotte "loved their kids, with affectionate words and touching—lots of hugging. You might say I learned to hug by hanging around the Day family.... In a real sense, Dick's family became the family I never had."[3]

The other major influence in Josh's recovery is his wife, Dottie. She always spoke with enthusiasm about her family; they meant everything to her. When Josh finally met Dottie's parents, he noticed the same qualities he had seen in his friends, Dick and Charlotte Day. Josh learned from Dottie's father "all kinds of things about what it means to be a loving husband and father.... He was always encouraging his kids, affirming them, and showing them he cared."[4] Josh McDowell remains enthusiastic about his family, devotes much of his spare time to his wife, and still gives lots of hugs.

Growing up in a home where Mom and Dad deeply love each other is the best way to learn how to love. But we can with God's help overcome even the most dysfunctional family history. He is a gracious God who can help parents to rise above a painful past. Both Josh McDowell and his friend Dick Day are evidence of that truth. You can provide a heritage of parental love for your children. It is within your reach.

HOW TO GROW MORE DEEPLY IN LOVE

How do we grow in the depth of our love? There are many good books and Web sites that can serve as resources on the subject. (See the resources section of this book for suggestions.) Seminars, retreats, and renewal weekends can be helpful. Couples in troubled marriages may also find help in counseling. There is no lack of resources available to couples. But a large number of marriages remain at risk. Many of them end in divorce.

Parents can get a divorce, but our kids can't. What happens to them when parents split? They cry and "stuff" the hurt. There it festers, destined eventually to reemerge—sometimes explosively.

Couples tend to dismiss the spiritual issues in their relationship. Psychological counseling may help, but what we need may be something much deeper. We must not allow the glib advice of well-meaning friends who offer such tired counsel as "just pray about it" or "let go and let God" to blind us to the true remedy. The answer may indeed be spiritual. We find lasting answers to every human need in one place and one person, the Lord Jesus Christ.

Allow me to offer some practical disciplines that build the kind of loving home for which every couple—and every child—longs.

THE DISCIPLINE OF PRAYER

"Bill and I need to see you, but I doubt that there is much that can be done. We fight over everything. I guess we just aren't compatible." I was surprised to hear Cathy's hopeless evaluation. I'd gone through premarital counseling with them and officiated at their wedding just two years ago. They were a couple of high quality, and I never figured I'd ever hear her say those words.

During our first meeting the couple seemed to engage in a quarrel of silence. I tried to breach the silence by asking them each to summarize their problems. No big difficulties emerged. They just seemed bored with one another. They even thought a divorce would benefit their son, Billy. "Billy will suffer less if we have the divorce while he is still an infant. It will be easier that way—easier for him and for us," Bill said.

Their callous indifference to each other, to their child's best interests, and to a watching world angered me. I did something I rarely do—I rebuked them. "You embarrass me! Where is that committed love we discussed so thoroughly in the premarital counseling sessions? I think you also embarrass our Lord Jesus Christ. I know you are both saved, but you're acting as though the Lord Jesus has done nothing for you. You're despising His work and His will. You're about to break this most sacred relationship of marriage and neither of you seem to care a snap about it. You'd have to be both blind and ignorant not to know that Billy needs you both...."

I kept up the pressure until Bill's eyes brimmed with tears. Cathy saw his tears, and she also began to sob quietly. I backed off and waited.

Bill broke the silence. "What can we do? We didn't plan it this way. It's just a lot of little things and I guess we're both spoiled and stubborn! I know a lot of it is my fault. I miss the freedom of my single days."

Before they left that day, we charted a course for rebuilding their marriage. The cornerstone for that process would be the discipline of daily prayer. They agreed to pray together each day for God to bless their marriage. Each was to ask the Lord for help to meet the other's needs. Each was to ask God to anchor in them a committed love that would refuse to give up. It worked. Today they are grandparents and still together. The most beneficial discipline for any marriage is prayer.

If you want to learn to love your spouse, pray. Ask God for the ability to see your spouse as His gift. Pray for patience, the will to forgive, and to love your spouse as God loves you. And pray *with* your spouse.

Whenever I counsel struggling couples, I always ask if they pray daily together for God to bless their marriage. The answer never changes. They don't. If they desire to continue in counseling with me, they must agree to pray daily together that God would strengthen their marriage. Otherwise, I terminate our counseling relationship.

Whenever a couple agrees to pray together, big problems tend to melt away. I have sometimes received more credit for my counsel than I deserve. The biggest factor in my counseling success is the God who answers prayers. It is presumptuous to assume that God will bless our marriages without continually asking Him to do so.

There are several different kinds of prayer a couple should regularly practice.

Fasting. Fervency in prayer often expresses itself through fasting. When we fast, we tell God we desire His intervention more than food. If health permits, fasting can be a powerful tool in prayer. No Christian couple should ever seek divorce without at least one partner fasting and praying for the Lord to heal their broken relationship. (Preferably both partners would be involved in this process.) Periodic fasts of one to three days honor the Lord and can bring miraculous answers.

Daily prayer. Marriage is a spiritual relationship. Every Christian couple needs to set apart a time to pray together. Ask the Lord to enable each of you to complement your spouse's needs. But never use your prayer time to preach. Establish a rule that each will only pray for the Lord's help to make each a better marriage partner. Reserve your prayer about the negatives for your private prayer. Pray together instead for the big positives—God's blessing on your marriage.

Prevailing prayer. Couples should together read prayers that are effective in spiritual warfare. Anita and I do this daily. We stay attentive and alert by reading aloud alternating paragraphs of the same kinds of prayers you find in this book. Prevailing prayers will keep couples alert to spiritual attack in their marriage.

Family prayer. Healthy families need daily family prayer times. Use this time to thank the Lord as a family for all that's good within your marriage and family. Reach out for more of God's goodness as a family. This will teach your children the value of prayer in marriage and family relationships.

THE DISCIPLINE OF BIBLICAL FINANCIAL MANAGEMENT

The additional resources section of this book includes readings that deal with the financial issues of the Christian life. Money is a major source of stress in marriages. A proper approach to financial management is essential to a strong marriage. I have three basic suggestions for wise management of the resources God entrusts to us.

1. Practice percentage giving. Financial matters in a Christian home require a focus on God. When we give to the

Lord the first portion of our income, He quickly becomes our focus. When He receives the first portion of our income, He also receives our praise as our resources increase. We then gain confidence in prayer because we know that *He* knows He is first in our lives. Extravagant purchases decline. Budgeting becomes an adventure and a joy as God prospers us and enables us to give even more than the first tenth of our income.

When we tithe, we have the flexibility to direct our generosity to areas of great need. And best of all, a Christian couple's focus is on their treasures in heaven rather than earthly riches.

Anita and I were married two years before we learned the discipline of tithing. Our would-be tithe money went toward sending a "poor boy" through school. Mark Bubeck was getting a seminary education, but God wasn't blessing our self-centered focus.

A number of factors combined to show us God had a better way. Unexpected doctor bills, traffic fines, broken typewriters (remember those?) to name just a few crises, found us at the end of every month with a negative cash flow. My wife and I finally sat down for dinner with a church elder and his family. We had noticed that our tiny church of thirty members consistently collected large offerings every week. I decided during dinner to ask my companion to explain the large offerings.

"We all tithe!" he said. "Even the children and young people give at least a tenth of their income every week. We share testimonies of how the Lord is blessing us in our personal finances and we're all learning that you cannot outgive God." On the way home that afternoon Anita and I decided to begin a lifetime habit of tithing. God has never disappointed us.

2. Develop a simple, workable budget. It will require some planning to create a budget that will enable you to pay all the bills each month. Begin by keeping good financial records to see where all your money goes. Then develop a simple budget to control your spending (and perhaps your lifestyle). The primary reason why so many couples end up broke is that they fail to establish a budget.

3. Avoid credit card purchases. Unless you are able to pay off the balance each month, you should avoid using credit cards. Credit cards can ruin more than budgets. They ruin marriages. They tend to charge exorbitant interest rates and encourage people to practice the idolatry of materialism.

THE DISCIPLINE OF GOOD COMMUNICATION AND CONFLICT RESOLUTION

I once counseled a couple that sought a divorce less than twelve months after their wedding. The husband had struck her and was reeling under guilt and shame. "I can't believe I would ever hit any woman, let alone my lovely wife!" he sobbed, his eyes overflowing with tears. "It frightens me to realize how I lost control." His wife, however, was not sure she wanted the marriage to continue. "Do you think you can help me, Pastor?" He was desperate.

What caused the blowup? Poor communication skills were at the root. Even during minor disagreements, they would refuse to talk with each other. One time they quarreled over whether they would sleep with their bedroom window opened or closed. But they wouldn't discuss it. He needed fresh air to sleep; she was always cold.

A power struggle developed. She felt that if he really loved her, it wouldn't matter if he were comfortable when they slept. He figured that if she really respected him, she would adjust to his needs. Poor communication and weak conflict resolution skills led them to the brink of divorce. She exploded when he left his dirty socks on the floor. He complained about her cooking. Even when they weren't arguing, the issues churned beneath the surface. Unresolved anger developed into bitterness. Finally, in the midst of an argument, he impulsively struck his wife.

Communication is never easy, even in the strongest marriage. It wasn't until this young couple came to a counselor that they found their answer. They purchased an electric blanket with dual controls. The most important lesson they needed to learn was to communicate. With loving respect for each other's views, any Christian couple can learn to do this. Couples need to develop a safe and positive environment in which differences can be discussed. Sometimes *mediated* clear-the-air sessions can help couples get past their own viewpoints and start thinking objectively.[5]

When we give in to sinful anger, we open the door for the evil works of our Adversary. If we justify our resentments or fail to discuss areas of disagreement, the Devil will soon take advantage of the opportunity. (See Eph. 4:26–27.) Communication between husband and wife is a *spiritual* matter. Work on your communication, and you will go a long way toward overcoming the Adversary in your home.

The Discipline of Removing Relational Barriers

Sometimes the cause of poor communication is a spiritual battle. Satan will do everything in his power to sabotage our marriages. He wants to disrupt communication and destroy biblical harmony so our families will self-destruct. But we often fail to recognize this obvious tactic. We find ourselves fighting each other instead of the real Enemy.

Carol telephoned me, bemoaning her difficult relationship with her husband. "It seems like there is a wall separating us. I never feel close to him anymore. There seems to be a barrier between us. I can communicate with everyone except Tom!"

A chief strategy of war has always been to disrupt the enemy's lines of communication. Armed forces must maintain reliable communications or they will soon take aim at each other. Carol's description of the barrier between her and Tom is a prime example of that strategy. No spiritual truth is more important than this simple yet profound statement: Satan's warfare strategy is to destroy relationships. We must aggressively and continually resist this strategy of the Adversary.

I instructed Carol to recite several times daily the following resistance prayer. I had previously counseled her and she replied, "Oh, you told me that before! How did I forget so quickly? I know that really works. I guess I was just so hurt that I forgot who was behind it. I'll get started again right away!" It didn't surprise me that Carol had forgotten the prayer. That's part of the Enemy's strategy. He wants to wound us to the point that we forget the truth. Here is the prayer:

> *In the name of the Lord Jesus Christ and by the power of His blood, I demolish and pull down all walls, barriers, and relationships the powers of darkness are building between Tom and me. I will only accept relationships between Tom and me that the Holy Spirit has authored in the will of God.*

The benefits of this resistance prayer are twofold: It will help you and it will help your spouse, who may be unwilling or unable to think straight. Your spouse will nevertheless recognize the removal of the barrier that blocked communication.

THE DISCIPLINE OF HEALTHY SEXUAL INTIMACY

"Pastor Bubeck, I've wanted to talk to you for a long time, but I could never get up enough nerve to share my problem with you." John hesitated for a moment while he twisted uncomfortably in his chair. I empathized with John and tried to help him feel comfortable enough to share what was bothering him.

"I can understand that, John. I've had some things in my life that were so personal I couldn't face them, let alone share them with someone else. You must need to talk about it, though, or you wouldn't have scheduled this time together. Anything you share I will treat as a sacred trust in complete confidentiality. Let's pray that the Lord will give both of us wisdom."

After a pause for prayer, John breathed a sigh of relief and blurted out his burden. "I've had a big problem with masturbation since I was ten years old. I've never told anyone. I thought I would be over it when I married Betty, but I went back to the old habit within the first month of our marriage. I feel so guilty and ashamed. I've cried out to God to help me and I do better for a short time, but then I'm back at it. I don't know what to do, Pastor."

"Have you ever thanked the Lord for making you a sexual person, John?" I asked my startled friend.

"No. I'm sure I'm oversexed. I think about sex most of the time. Betty and I have a fairly good physical relationship together, except I feel so guilty about what I do. If she knew she'd be really hurt. She'd feel like she was a failure when I'm the one who's all messed up!"

Sexual intimacy is a discipline? you may be wondering. The answer is *Absolutely!* I have heard scores of stories just like John's. There are few areas in which we are more susceptible to Satan's attacks. Sexual defeats cause a high level of stress in the lives of sincere Christians. Guilt feelings, self-hatred, and despair are common reactions.

But as we begin to understand God's plan for this area of our identity we can regain health. Our sexuality is part of God's creative design. He made us sexual beings; there is nothing sinful about sexual desire. It becomes sinful when those desires find expression in unhealthy or immoral behavior patterns. Sexual sin comes in a variety of flavors, but our victory over it begins with thanksgiving to the Lord for the gift of sexuality.

God's plan for sexual expression in marriage is a spiritual matter. The intimacy of the physical union of marriage illustrates the intimacy that exists between Christ and His church.

Bible passages such as Ephesians 5:28–32 and 1 Corinthians 7:3–5 explain how we are to esteem our spouse and not withhold our bodies from that person with whom we have become one. The Bible elevates God's plan for sex to its proper spiritual level. It should be our prayer that the Lord would make our sexual encounters a "praise the Lord" experience as we enjoy His blessing.

Many of us approach marriage, however, with a polluted and corrupt understanding of sex. The world's perversity, reluctance on the part of Christian parents to discuss sexuality, and Satan's deliberate attempts to twist God's plan for sexual expression in marriage have undermined the spiritual nature of the sexual union. The Adversary desperately wants to corrupt the activity God uses as the preeminent illustration of intimacy between Christ and His church. Always remember that your sexual relationship with your spouse is a spiritual matter. Any lasting correction requires a kind of spiritual warfare prayer that resists and forbids any demonic corruption of the marital relationship. Please make it a sacred focus of your prayer life.

OTHER WAYS TO INCREASE MARITAL LOVE

The following additional suggestions may help you display more effectively your love for your mate.

Daily bestow verbalized blessings. Beyond saying a simple "thank you," learn to commend your spouse for a job well done, proper attitudes, and loving help.

Practice the communication of touch. "I love it when you come up to me, put your arm around my waist and hug me," my wife said just this week. After forty-five years of marriage, we still love to touch and be touched. Without a word a touch can say, "I love you; you're important to me; I need to know you are near me."

From the moment of a baby's birth, the cuddling and touching of a mother and father communicate tender, loving care to their child. Appropriate and affectionate touches and embraces are important avenues that communicate love throughout a child's life, and our appreciation for affectionate touch doesn't wane when we reach adulthood.

Touching and caressing are important to the love act of marriage, but don't forget that simple touches, absent any sexual agenda, also powerfully convey the love we feel.

Ask forgiveness. I can't remember being closer to Anita than when I have had to ask for her forgiveness. Times of confession and forgiveness are intimate and emotional experiences of spiritual significance. We communicate in those times a deep reverence for God, love for our spouse, humility of heart, and spiritual maturity. To ask forgiveness is essential to a healthy Christian marriage.

Make deliberate choices to please your spouse. The cross represents the immeasurably high price Christ was willing to pay for our redemption. The message of the cross is one of love without limits. Though it was a painful and repulsive death reserved for criminals, nothing could turn Him aside from going to the cross. He went voluntarily, because of His love for us.

The message of the cross enhances the intimacy and oneness of marriage. A loving spouse will do things he doesn't want to do and will go places he doesn't want to go. A loving wife will shiver by her husband's side at a football game when it's the last place on earth she would choose to be. She is there, not because she loves football, but because she wants to please him. A loving husband may go to the symphony or some banquet, not out of a love for music or "rubber chicken" dinners and speakers who drone on too long, but because his first interest is his wife. When we act selflessly with a pleasant smile, it becomes a spiritual ministry to our spouse.

THE ROLE OF COMMITMENT IN LOVING YOUR SPOUSE

Biblical love is committed love. It even embraces people who don't want us to love them. Committed love in marriage eliminates the word *divorce* from the Christian's vocabulary. Only then can marriage truly become "for better or for worse." Committed love transcends divorce.

That does not mean we should just hunker down and endure a miserable marriage. It does not mean we should cloak ourselves in a martyr's robe of suffering and pain. It means that no matter how challenging marriage becomes, we should persevere in prayer, hope, effort, and sacrifice to make it work. Even if separation and intense survival efforts are necessary, the commitment should remain.

Doug and Terri had a broken marriage. With his numerous adulterous affairs, Doug had betrayed their wedding vows and Terri ordered him to leave. Though that drastic action necessitated the sale of their home and relocation to another city, Terri was convinced it was her only option. Counseling sessions seemed fruitless and Doug's promises to change were empty. Deception, involvement with other women, and suspicious expenditures proved too much for Terri. The hurt, anger, and frustration convinced her that separation was necessary for her survival. Doug and Terri couldn't even stay together for the sake of their young children. They needed some space.

Doug landed a job in another city and began intensive counseling with a Christian therapist both he and Terri trusted. The shock of his loss delivered a dose of reality he had never known. He was determined to find answers for the defeat that was ripping apart his life.

Terri and the children moved in with her parents. She found a job and began to build a new life for herself and her children. Her hurt, anger, and fear rendered off limits any talk of reconciliation. Terri couldn't bear the thought of allowing Doug to once again betray her trust, but she still did not see divorce as a viable option. She realized the Lord hates divorce, and she believed it would ultimately do the children more harm than good. Terri's commitment to her marriage vows also ruled out divorce. Unless Doug sought a divorce, they would remain married but separated.

Months passed. Hope of reconciliation was nonexistent; their occasional phone conversations usually ended with Terri venting her anger at Doug. The passage of time provided an interlude of rest and relief from all the conflict, but talk of reconciliation never came up.

Doug and Terri's committed love provided the only hope for their broken marriage. Both had opportunity to pursue other personal involvements, but commitment protected each from allowing that to happen. Neither considered divorce an option. Though they had no answer for their frustrated and broken marriage, they both remained committed. With the passing of time and prayerful intercession by Christian parents and friends, the Lord restored their marriage. Marital counseling, patience, and committed love worked. They have gone on to rebuild a strong marriage. Their children are growing up in an intact family with the love and support of both parents.

One of the tragedies of divorce is the way it has trampled committed love. When hurt, betrayal, and anger are acute, people often seek revenge. The rubble it produces includes not only marriage partners who will never fully recover, but also wounded children who will bear scars for the rest of their lives. With a little hard work and painful endurance, this tragedy can be avoided even in the most dire circumstances. Romantic love has an important place in marriage, but without a commitment to back it up, romance eventually proves inadequate. Romantic love is centered on emotion. Committed love involves both the mind and the will. Commitment is a spiritual gift of God, and it is a reflection of His love for us. For a healthy marriage, commitment is a spiritual necessity.

THE SPIRITUAL NECESSITIES OF MARRIAGE

Growing love in our marriage requires us to remember and practice the eleven spiritual necessities to marriage we have considered in this chapter. They are as follows:

- Daily prayer together for God to bless the marriage
- A biblical approach to financial management
- Effective communication and conflict resolution skills
- The removal of relational barriers
- Sexual fulfillment according to God's design
- Resistance to the Adversary's plans
- The daily practice of verbally blessing our spouse
- The daily practice of repeated *nonsexual* touching of our spouse
- The art of asking forgiveness
- The regular pursuit of activities our spouse enjoys (especially if it's something we *don't* enjoy)
- The practice of committed love

5

Parents Who Communicate

He had tears in his eyes. I'd seen my father cry only twice before. The first time was when he spanked me at age eleven. It was only the second time he had ever spanked me. I'd disobeyed him in a matter that had exposed my little brother to great danger. My dad applied the "board of education" to my "seat of learning," producing cries from me that were more emotional than physical. After it was over, I looked at Dad. Tears were streaming down his cheeks.

I never forgot. Communication. In those tears he communicated his love for me and that my punishment had been more painful for him than it was for me.

The second time I witnessed Dad cry was just before America entered World War II. December 7, 1941. Pearl Harbor. As a thirteen-year-old boy it moved me with emotion. I listened to every news report. What did it all mean? Looking for reassurance and comfort, I edged close to Dad. He stood looking out our backyard window. I edged around until I could look up at his eyes. I saw his tears.

I never forgot. Communication. In those tears he communicated his deep love for our country and its soldiers. His tears communicated concern for sons whom his country might send to war.

Now I was witnessing Dad cry for just the third time in my life. He and I had just placed the last bag of my belongings in the car. The truck we had borrowed carried the rest of my possessions. My bride of eleven months was by my side. We were headed toward seminary eight hundred miles away. It was time to say good-bye. Anita and I hugged and kissed Mom through all of her tears. She often shed them in emotional moments. I went to Dad. He had his back turned, gazing into our car's overflowing trunk. I extended my hand to Dad. He turned and revealed eyes streaming tears.

Communication! It showed me how much he cared.

Dad's caring love was deeply personal. He'd always done the hard, nasty things that sometimes needed doing on the farm. He wouldn't let his sons do those. Dad was also like that in times of danger. He communicated love by giving of himself. He demonstrated his commitment to the family and to the values in which he believed.

That's another way parents rear strong children who can confront the Adversary. Moms and dads can instruct by their words, but even more so by what they *do*. By their words and actions, parents teach love and devotion in a way that imparts not just a sense of right and wrong, but also a sense of security in a world that feels very unsafe.

TALK ABOUT GOD'S PRINCIPLES

Anita and I recently opened a family devotional guide that directed us to read Deuteronomy 6:1–9. There Moses commanded the people of Israel to follow the statutes and laws of

God. It struck me anew that God made parents responsible for the communication of His truth to the next generation. "These commandments that I give to you today are to be upon your hearts. Impress them on your children. Talk about them when you sit at home and when you walk along the road, when you lie down and when you get up" (Deut. 6:6–7).

God insists that parents must communicate truth to their children. We must first get the truth of God into our own hearts, then it must flow outward. We are to saturate our children with the diligent communication of God's truth.

Deuteronomy 6:6–7 places the communication of God's truth at the focal point of our teaching plan. Our conversational time with our children should skillfully integrate God's truth. When we sit in our homes, or take a leisurely walk, when we get ready for bed, and when we rise in the morning, we are to teach our children God's truth. Every aspect of our words and lives must communicate it.

The homeschooling of children has become popular among Christian parents. I used to be skeptical about homeschooling. My view has shifted 180 degrees. Skillful homeschooling represents a revolutionary improvement in the educational process. The major benefit of homeschooling is communication. The curriculum forces parents out of their silence. They have to talk with their children about important, meaningful things. It results in a profound closeness between child and parent, which is missing in this era of addiction to electronic media.

EXPRESS YOUR LOVE

Communication is vital in all areas, not just in our children's education. It affects relationships and, when it is tender and warm, builds trust, hope, and love among family members.

Conversely, ignoring opportunities for communication damages our relationships and our ability to prepare our children for adulthood.

The Barnharts were running into problems with their twelve-year-old son, Tommy. He showed signs of rebellion at school and at home. Tommy's alarmed parents asked me to see if I could get through to him. Tommy and I had always enjoyed a warm relationship. He loved to be around me. He would sometimes linger as I greeted people after the church service, hoping to catch my eye and receive some special attention.

When Tommy came into my office, he was sullen and withdrawn. He didn't want to talk. He resented his mom and dad for informing me about him. I told him his friendship meant a lot to me and that I had lately missed seeing him at the door of the church. A tear trickled from Tommy's eye. I waited.

Brokenhearted sobs suddenly erupted from deep inside. A torrent of confusion, hurt, and anger tumbled out. I learned that at the core of Tommy's problem was a lack of meaningful communication between him and his parents. It surprised me. Fred and Nancy Barnhart obviously deeply loved Tommy. Their sun rose and set on their children. Everyone knew that. But Tommy didn't.

Why? Because Dad didn't *show* his love, and Mom didn't *declare* her love. Fred never hugged Tommy. That didn't seem manly. Dad would watch his ball games but never complimented him. He instead told Tommy how he could have done it better. Mom never congratulated her son when his grades were good, but he heard about it if they were mediocre.

It was the old story of well-meaning parents unable to communicate with a sensitive son. A few important apologies and some corrected communication approaches transformed a situation headed for serious problems. A commitment to change communication patterns made a huge difference in that family.

If we are to transfer positive attitudes and principles to our children and grandchildren, loving communication must be present. There are several areas where this is especially important.

TWO KEY AREAS OF COMMUNICATION

SEXUALITY

Jim had a problem. He was addicted to pornography and at times engaged in fetish-associated masturbation. His marriage was in shambles. Though a believer, his sexual obsessions were destroying his credibility as a follower of Christ. What was wrong? Like many men, Jim grew up without one word from his parents about his sexuality. Neither Dad nor Mom ever breathed a word to him about his sexual drives. Jim consequently got the message that sex is a mysterious and powerful force that a man must repress.

Some may think this a strange place to begin when talking about areas of communication. But it is the most tragically neglected area of communication between Christian parents and their children. Our sexuality is one of God's greatest gifts. He created us to be either male or female. The expression of our sexuality in marriage is the means by which God blesses us with children and families. God designed it to enable married couples to experience intimacy and oneness of body, soul, and spirit. The apostle Paul, as we mentioned earlier, used the concept of sexual intimacy to illustrate the intimacy of Christ with His church. (See Eph. 5:21–23.)

Throughout my years of premarital counseling, more than 90 percent of those counseled said they had never received any meaningful information about their sexuality from either parent. The reluctance of most parents to discuss sex with their children is largely responsible for the distorted views of sexuality that currently run rampant in our culture. But what does it say to our children when we refuse them accurate and biblical information? Or worse yet, when out of our embarrassment we offer either misinformation or a vague answer? Children quickly learn that sex must indeed be a very dirty business. They get a message that says, "The best people I know can't talk to me about it." So instead of learning the beauty of God's plan from their parents, young men and women receive distorted and incomplete instruction from their peers or from some other authority figure who doesn't share their parents' Christian values.

A better way to approach this situation would be to carefully plan talks about sex that offer children a healthy view of their sexuality. This discussion should include a time to present age-appropriate materials that teach a biblical view of sexuality.

Such communication is essential. The Adversary is hunting for our kids, and one of his tactics is to distort human sexuality. Advertisers, the entertainment media, homosexual activists, and pornographic Internet sites exploit and distort sexuality in the pursuit of their agendas. Sexual predators are also proliferating in our culture. We must prepare our children to be on the alert to such people, and it begins with open communication from a Christian perspective. (See the resources listed under "Communicating Biblical Sexual Values.")

One of the Devil's chief strategies involves the corruption and perversion of human sexuality. Two motivations underlie this strategy. The first motivation is to dishonor the Lord Jesus Christ and His redemptive work. Satan understands that the sexual union illustrates the love of Christ for His church. The more that Satan is able to twist the idea of human sexuality, the more he is able to deface its beauty.

Satan's second motivation is to open a door of opportunity to subject people to demonic influence. In 1 Corinthians 6, the Lord offers insight as to why sex outside marriage is something we must resist at all costs.

> The body is not meant for sexual immorality, but for the Lord, and the Lord for the body.... Do you not know that your bodies are members of Christ himself? Shall I then take the members of Christ and unite them with a prostitute? Never! Do you not know that he who unites himself with a prostitute is one with her in body? For it is said, "The two will become one flesh." ... Flee from sexual immorality. All other sins a man commits are outside his body, but he who sins sexually sins against his own body. (vv. 13, 15–16, 18)

In the sexual union of a man and woman, two people become "one flesh." The consequences are far-reaching. When that bond takes place in an inappropriate and immoral fashion, it establishes a bond that may open one's life to demonic powers, powers that can stake an active claim against a person. This bond occurs regardless of the type of sexual activity. That is perhaps one reason why God pronounces such severe judgment on sexual sins. It also provides insight into why the Lord forbade intermarriage of His people with pagan, idolatrous cultures.

Spiritual Salvation

One other topic of communication can lead your children to a place where they are able to resist the Adversary. Talk with them about their spiritual needs. Parents need to watch over their children's spiritual development and give them clear opportunities to respond to Christ's call to salvation.

Look for occasions when your children are ready to make a decision to receive the Lord Jesus Christ as their personal Savior. Pray. But do not spiritually bludgeon your children with their need for salvation. Remember, it is the Holy Spirit's responsibility to work in each child's life. Parental teaching is in order but not parental manipulation. We must rely on God to draw our children to salvation. We do not want to manufacture an inauthentic decision that will not stand the test of time. The new birth is not an effect of parental persuasion. Its source is the Holy Spirit.

I remember a boy whose parents prayed but did not badger their son about his lost spiritual condition. They provided all their children with consistent teaching about the need for the Savior. Christian education, camp experiences, and regular exposure to biblical preaching were part of his upbringing. The instrument God used to draw him to Christ at the age of eight was the vacation Bible school at their church.

He was a mischievous, fun-loving kid; not someone you'd expect to be attentive to the Lord's prompting. The message of salvation and the Holy Spirit's power were at work. On the final day of Bible school, the two teachers gave a public invitation to receive Christ as Savior. That classroom became as quiet as a cathedral. Several girls went forward but no boys.

The young lad struggled. Yes, I was that eight-year-old. God was drawing me. My heart was pounding. His conviction was personal and deep. I stood up and walked to the front. The Lord removed my sense of guilt, and a peace flooded my inner being. I knew something wonderful had happened. I told my mother, who was both pleased and surprised. After all, I had publicly responded to a gospel invitation just the previous year.[1]

Genuine conversion makes everything new. I still struggled, as we all do, with sin. But a fundamental change had taken place. Parents, remember that your child's need for a real relationship with God is the most basic preparation for a stable walk in this world. It should be a primary part of parenting communication.

HOW TO SAY "I LOVE YOU"

Communication that says "I love you" imparts security and builds a healthy sense of self. At the Bubeck household, my wife and I compose a poem every year for each of our nine grandchildren. They get their poem from Grandma and Grandpa Bubeck on their birthday. It's been part of our family tradition since my kids were small.

I wanted to find a way I could individually communicate a caring love to each of them. God led me to write original poetry. The tradition continues to this day. Every family member—my wife, three daughters, three sons-in-law, and nine grandchildren—enjoys reading those poems. That requires effort, but there is a huge payoff. I seek to communicate through those poems the truth of both God's and my own caring love. My 1995 poem to my granddaughter Christie ended with the following:

> Happy, Happy Birthday! To our Christie precious pearl!
> Though you may be growing fast you're still our little
> girl
> Who's won our hearts with your love and happy little face ...
> Lord, do keep our little Christie for many birthdays
> more,
> And bless her with all good things from Your blessings store;

> Keep her humble in her beauty and gracious in her
> ways,
> Fill her heart with strong faith and teach her as she
> prays
> To be like Jesus as she grows in maturity and grace
> Until He comes again and we see His blessed face!

How do you communicate love to your children? You may not be a poet, but "I love you" can take many forms. Whatever creative way you choose, your children need to hear that message on a regular basis. Healthy emotional and spiritual well-being requires our regular expression of love.

I have listed below many suggestions that may help you to communicate caring love to children of all ages. But don't stop with them. Develop your own list and make them a part of your regular practice.

SAYING "I LOVE YOU" TO PRESCHOOL-AGE CHILDREN

- ❑ Hug and touch in appropriate ways.
- ❑ Express age-appropriate words of love and interest.
- ❑ Read to your preschooler while holding him in your lap.
- ❑ Play age-appropriate games with your preschool child. (And let her win!)
- ❑ Write cards and craft celebrations that emphasize how you value your children.
- ❑ Pray aloud short, meaningful prayers that communicate your loving concern.
- ❑ Participate with your children in activities they enjoy.
- ❑ Talk face-to-face on a regular basis with your children.
- ❑ Compliment your child's appearance and positive character traits. Correct behavior, but emphasize her essential worth.

▫ Discover ways to communicate caring love in a way that recognizes and honors your child's unique gifts.

SAYING "I LOVE YOU" TO GRADE-SCHOOL-AGE CHILDREN:

▫ Hug them. Guard against touches that could be interpreted as sexual in nature.

▫ Read to them age-appropriate books. Bible storybooks are great. If suitable, read to a younger child as he or she sits on your lap.

▫ Display interest in your child's studies, sports activities, and hobbies.

▫ Verbalize your love and respect. "I love you, Mary! You're important to me." Or "I love you, Jack. I think you're a great kid."

▫ Take your child to the mall or somewhere that is of interest to him.

▫ Listen to their concerns and help them to resolve conflict with their friends in a biblical manner.

▫ Help your child with difficult school assignments.

▫ Pray aloud for your child. Pray for his or her future spouse and for his or her choice of occupation.

▫ Honor your children on such special events as birthdays and other celebrations. Pay attention to their spiritual needs.

▫ Maintain eye contact in conversation with your child.

COMMUNICATING LOVE TO ADOLESCENTS

Sometimes we think older children don't need to hear the words "I love you." After all, they are older, and they already know we love them. We say to ourselves, "They've seen it." It's true that our verbal expressions of love to a teenager may elicit an embarrassed silence or an "Aw, Mom!"—especially when we say it in public. But all kids want to know they're loved—even more so as they move through adolescence, and self-doubts plague them and desires for acceptance increase. There are many ways to express our love in nonverbal ways. Build on the list I've provided, and begin to communicate caring love at a meaningful level to your child.

SAYING "I LOVE YOU" TO MIDDLE-SCHOOL-AGE CHILDREN

❏ Honor individuality. If he enjoys hugs, great. But don't offend and embarrass him if he thinks he's beyond that.

❏ Listen to his issues and concerns. If some new trend is unacceptable to you, take the time to explain why, offering compelling reasons. Set fair, defined limits and expectations.

❏ Reassure your daughter often that she is beautiful in both appearance and character qualities.

❏ Plan meaningful and fun activities in which she will want to participate with the whole family.

❏ Set aside meaningful times for deeper talks about life choices and decisions. Go to a coffee shop and treat him or her to a latte. Attend a family conference with your child. It may promote some interesting discussions.

❏ Include your son's closest friends in an activity of his choosing. Acceptance of his friends and influencing them toward the Lord is something he will appreciate.

❏ Build on the caring concern you've previously set by continuing to pray often for the spouse God has planned for him. Tell him you are praying that he will remain sexually pure for his future spouse.

❏ Exercise age-appropriate discipline that honors your child's dignity and does not demean his or her self-worth.

◻ Commend your child often for character development, significant accomplishments, and spiritual virtues.

◻ Watch for ways to help your child know that you think your spouse is your best friend. Observing your love for his other parent will also allow him to sense your love for him.

SAYING "I LOVE YOU" TO HIGH-SCHOOL-AGE CHILDREN

◻ Set regular times that are conducive to talking about important topics. Breakfast or lunch dates, trips to a coffee shop, etc. Such appointments communicate value.

◻ Apologize (when appropriate) to your high-school student concerning wrong decisions or actions you've made. Be transparent in your confession of your inappropriate attitudes.

◻ Convey your desire to honor her as a young adult who can come to you as a counselor and guidance resource. Let her know that at this stage you still retain veto power on issues you consider very important.

◻ Hug your teenage child and verbalize often your love for him.

◻ Watch for ways to communicate caring love by spur of the moment e-mails, special greeting cards, gifts, and special recognitions.

◻ Provide a list of colleges and universities that you find acceptable. Ask your high-school student to begin to pray and investigate which college might be the one God wants him or her to attend.

◻ Pray for God to keep your teen sexually pure for his or her future spouse.

◻ Discuss professional and vocational choices, as well as gifts and abilities that you've noticed in him or her.

- Maintain eye contact during your conversations at all times.

- Let your teen hear you pray about stressful times, tests, personal relationships, and any other personal concerns that you may carry.

THE PLACE OF DISCIPLINE AND DUTY IN LOVE

"Don't hold back on the mower, Luke. Let it do the work. You just guide it where it's supposed to go. That's better. You're doing great." Those were my words to my ten-year-old grandson as I spent the better part of an hour helping him learn how to mow the lawn. He wasn't a fast learner. It was, in fact, a real effort for him to pay attention and to follow the mower. I was in a hurry to get back to my writing. *Should I end the lesson and just do it myself?* I thought. After all, the exercise would be good for me. I nearly forgot the most basic essential of communication: patience.

The Lord reminded me that patience is one of the evidences of a Spirit-filled life. I paused and asked the Holy Spirit to grant me patience and to calm my spirit. My grandson and I finished our little lawn care lesson and enjoyed some quality time together.

When we lovingly administer discipline and supervise tasks, we communicate love at a life-enriching level. It's one of the ways our Lord communicates His love to believers: "The Lord disciplines those he loves" (Heb. 12:6). Proper discipline communicates deep love. It shows we really care.

Teach your child to differentiate between right and wrong. Parents are to be the primary communicators of values. Don't be afraid to express those values, and don't shield your child from the consequences of poor choices. He may get angry, but your child will eventually thank you. Loving discipline is the key that unlocks the door to maturity.

Proper discipline of children requires planning, timing, and patience. The teaching of responsibility requires both instruction and accountability. We successfully transfer our values when we instruct our children and hold them accountable. If our children don't learn responsibility and accountability from us, they're heading toward a disaster.

I was six years old when Dad assigned me the task of milking a certain cow both morning and night. The only excuse for skipping this task was illness. He checked on me often to see if I'd done it well. When I did a good job, Dad commended and encouraged me. A poor job meant Dad would call me back to the barn to do it right.

That was the way Dad did things. He pushed his sons to their limits. There were times it would have been easier to do it himself. But he understood his role as a teacher of discipline and accountability. Today I'm grateful. That's where I developed a strong work ethic that has served me well over the years.

Talk to your children about duties and responsibilities. Hold them accountable. It will be inconvenient to check their work and occasionally call them back to redo the task, but you will help them gain maturity and dependability.

TALKING ABOUT HARMFUL INFLUENCES

Our youngest daughter, Judy, suffered panic attacks as a young girl. Judy's symptoms, which peaked at age eleven, included nausea and painful colitis, which produced fear and confusion. The medical community had no answers for us. We considered the need for psychotherapy. But we eventually suspected that the problem was a spiritual attack on our daughter. We dealt directly with the powers of darkness that we suspected were oppressing our daughter. The result was an immediate deliverance.

Judy's trial reminded me of the need to counsel our children to avoid harmful influences. Several years after Judy experienced deliverance from her nausea and panic, she shared with me some significant information. Prior to those attacks, Judy had attended a sleepover with friends where they experimented with levitation, a crude séance, a Ouija board, and extrasensory perception (ESP). The spiritual attacks began shortly after her brief experience with the occult.

Harmful influences threaten to undermine our children's growth into mature and secure adults. We need to talk with our children about those influences. It doesn't require a lecture, but we do need to deal directly with the issues. We need to explain to our children the dangers that threaten their well-being. For our daughter Judy it was the occult. The Adversary is on the prowl. The servants of the Adversary will influence our children in any way they can: with music, the media, and peer pressure. Let's look at each of these.

SPIRITISTIC AND OCCULT INFLUENCES

How did our daughter Judy get involved in harmful occult influence? Simple. We had never warned her about such things. We had never dreamed we'd need to concern ourselves with protecting our innocent, young daughter from occult influences. We were wrong.

Another one of our daughters had in her youth engaged in similar occult experimentation. Both daughters later experienced considerable pain that resulted from their youthful curiosity.

We learned important lessons from those episodes, but I deeply regret my ignorance of the danger that stalked my kids. The influences of spiritism and the occult have exploded in our culture. Many different flavors of spiritism now appear in books, movies, on the Internet, and in computer games.

Public schools and colleges encourage spiritistic experimentation. Many children's toys have their beginning in pagan and occult myths. It's everywhere. Christian parents must warn their children about the dangers of these things. We dare not leave our children in ignorance. Their spiritual well-being depends on our diligence.

How should a concerned parent communicate adequate warning? The Bible contains the best answer. Allow the Word of God to speak for itself. Plan a time when you can talk separately with each child. Inform him or her of the proliferation of spiritistic messages. Explain how seemingly innocent and playful experiences of supernatural and so-called *paranormal* phenomena actually mask the true dangers of these spiritual phenomena. You will want to examine Scripture with your child. A great text to read is Deuteronomy 18:9–12 (NKJV):

> When you come into the land which the LORD your God is giving you, you shall not learn to follow the abominations of those nations. There shall not be found among you anyone who makes his son or his daughter pass through the fire, or one who practices witchcraft, or a soothsayer, or one who interprets omens, or a sorcerer, or one who conjures spells, or a medium, or a spiritist, or one who calls up the dead. For all who do these things are an abomination to the LORD, and because of these abominations the LORD your God drives them out from before you.

This should remove any doubt that spiritistic experimentation is dangerous. You may want to investigate the meaning of words such as *sorcerer, abomination,* and *spiritist.* A standard dictionary will provide a concise definition, and a Bible dictionary or commentary will offer deeper biblical insight. The broad, inclusive warning of Deuteronomy 18 should satisfy most questions about the spiritistic experimentation that has captured the attention of so many.

Another useful biblical passage is Ephesians 5:6–8; 11–13.

> Because of such things God's wrath comes on those who are disobedient. Therefore do not be partners with them. For you were once darkness, but now you are light in the Lord. Live as children of light.... Have nothing to do with the fruitless deeds of darkness, but rather expose them. For it is shameful even to mention what the disobedient do in secret. But everything exposed by the light becomes visible.

Children gain an advantage when they understand why they should avoid contemporary expressions of spiritism. It will strengthen them to resist the pressure of their peers.

MEDIA INFLUENCES

Media have the potential to convey useful and healthy information, entertainment, and social awareness. Media are, in and of themselves, neutral. It is those who control the media who determine the content. Their worldview colors the information they transmit to us. We have the obligation to both monitor and discuss its content with our children.

Most television sets now contain a V-chip to help parents restrict access to certain programming based on that program's violence and maturity rating. All a parent has to do is to set the V-chip to a particular rating, and it will provide some protection against inappropriate material.

We must communicate our love by warning our children about negative media influences and by helping them to guard against the Adversary who threatens to rob them of their innocence. There are several influences that we must be aware of in the lives of our children.

Music. Encourage your kids to be aware of lyrics, performers' lifestyles, and the seductive pressures that exist in the world of contemporary music culture. Music can serve as a gateway to involvement in the occult. A helpful rating system that discloses the nature of the recording's lyrics is now in place. But it is also a good idea for parents to help their children objectively evaluate the music they hear.

Parents must take the initiative to provide helpful tools for their kids to use in evaluating music and other media while their children remain open to their influence.[2] Music has the power to shape both habits and worldviews. It can inspire a child to greatness or reduce him to baseness. Parents must seize the opportunity to use music as an uplifting, inspiring tool that reinforces godly values and honors the Lord.

Movies, television, and cartoons. With the availability of cable and satellite subscriptions, the variety of television programming is expanding at an exponential rate. Some television programs can serve as excellent educational tools and family-friendly allies. There are, however, many programs that see it as their mission to ridicule and deconstruct the family or to promote occult and neo-pagan themes. The more indulgent our culture becomes, the more parents must exercise protective oversight. To do otherwise will be to open the door to the Adversary.

And what about movies? The movie industry employs a rating system that has, unfortunately, become virtually worthless. Even G and PG movies often contain New Age themes. And you might as well forget about the PG-13 option. All it means is that they *probably* won't view any gratuitous nudity and will hear *fewer* of the profanities that have become common fare in popular culture. The wide availability of DVDs and the appearance of digital video recorders (DVRs) also makes it quite a challenge to monitor what our kids watch. So, what's a parent to do?

When your son or daughter asks permission to go to a movie or rent a DVD, ask some questions. Answers to these questions should help you determine if you want your child watching a particular show.

- Does the movie or music video under consideration promote fear, vulgar language, or disrespect for authority?
- Are there unbiblical, supernatural, or occult themes?
- Does the presentation glorify death, bloodshed, and a disrespect for life?
- Does the showing present a view of sexuality or family relationships that undermines a Christian worldview?
- Does the movie endorse or subtly encourage involvement in occult or spiritistic activity?
- Is the movie or video respectful of Christianity?
- Does it display or encourage the development of the fruit of the Spirit? (See Gal. 5:22–23.)

Public-school curriculum. We live in a pluralistic society that encourages children to explore any value or faith system *other* than Christianity. Even the few institutions that claim to teach moral values do so not on the basis of Judeo-Christian values, but according to "community standards." Some public-school systems even include in their curriculum New Age and spiritistic methods of relaxation and visualization. Textbooks contain stories featuring witches and the occult. The talented and gifted curriculum in my grandson's Iowa classroom instructs elementary schoolers to "totally empty your mind of all distractions" and to "watch now for someone who is coming to help you. Let him lead you."

What can Christian parents do about the inclusion of such occult and New Age themes in public-school programs? Christian schools or homeschooling may be an answer. That may not be an option for everyone, however. Finances, abilities, and time limitations may necessitate public school for many Christian parents.

Here are four guidelines that deserve consideration:

▫ Seek information by carefully listening to your children's reports on school life.

▫ Ask what he is learning, then respond to ideas he hears in the classroom. Be sure you remain the principal communicator of truth in your child's life.

▫ Teach your children to discern truth from error in the curriculum of the public school. Build into them an awareness of flaws inherent in evolutionary theory, moral permissiveness, opposition to prayer, and secular humanism.

▫ Become an appropriate activist. Influence public-school decisions by respectfully telling school officials and teachers about practices and curricula you consider detrimental to your children.

PEER PRESSURE

Peer pressure is one of life's real challenges. The desire for approval and acceptance is universal. One way to render our children less vulnerable to peer pressure is to discuss with them their value as people and to remind them of your love. If your child is particularly sensitive, this will be a challenge that requires continual reinforcement. Help them to see that *your* approval and *God's* approval are more valuable than the approval of their peers.

A child's peers can be cruel. Al was vulnerable to peer pressure as a boy. He always wanted to please and gain acceptance. His vulnerability made him the object of pranks and humiliation by his peers. On one occasion they dug a hole in the woods and filled it with worms and small snakes.

Then as a practical joke, they lured him into the woods and tossed him into the hole just to hear his screams of terror. Al had an abnormal fear of worms and snakes when he was a child. Now as an adult, his aversion is severe: A sidewalk worm after a rainfall can send him running in the opposite direction. Rage and anger accompany the panic attacks.

I still get angry when I think of that story. It reminds me how ruthless peer pressure can be. Some of life's greatest cruelties happen in the guise of play. If anything should convince us of the depravity of humankind, it's the cruelty children often display toward each other.

Peer pressure is serious business. Display great empathy with your children. They need to know their parents understand how peer pressure affects them. There are some specific ways we can encourage and equip our children to be strong in the face of peer pressure.

Tell true stories that illustrate the rewards of standing firm in your beliefs. Help your children to appreciate the virtues of courage and conviction. The Bible story of Daniel and his three friends is a great one to share. Other true stories from the Bible as well as from contemporary life can promote this virtue.

Discuss the issue of peer pressure with your children early and often. Pray with and for your children about the pressures they face. Listen empathetically to their struggles and don't dismiss them by saying, "You should just ignore them." Instead, take time to praise them for their stand. Ask them how they feel, and then listen. Pray with them, asking God to give them the courage to stand for what is right.

I began this chapter with a description of my dad's tears, which communicated clearly his love for me as well as for others. You can communicate your love just as clearly. It doesn't require shedding crocodile tears. And it's not higher math. All it requires is a genuine love and a willingness to express it to your children as they navigate the issues of life.

It all boils down to a determination to reflect God's communication with us. God demonstrated His love when He became one of us. We saw it as Jesus healed the sick, cleansed the lepers, wept at Lazarus's tomb, and raised the dead to life. But it wasn't until they lifted Him up on the cross at Golgotha's hill that each of us really understood: God *really* loves me. He took what I deserved. He paid for my sins. He rose again to fill me with resurrection life. He *communicated!* He still does. The saving grace of our Lord Jesus Christ gives life and hope to all who believe.

Part 3

BREAKING THE GRIP
OF THE ADVERSARY

6

Setting Our Children Free

Why are you reading this book? Perhaps you're a parent with a problem child. You're wondering if you are reaping a delayed harvest. Maybe you're a new Christian with a rough past, and you're wondering if it might be the wisest choice not to have a family. It may be that you and your spouse struggle with infertility. You want to adopt but question whether it's safe to rear a child in this world. Or maybe you're a Christian leader, and you want to know how best to help people whose children are breaking their hearts. You want to help them avoid that delayed harvest and lead their children into a life of spiritual victory, fulfillment, and freedom.

Let me assure you: God knows all about your needs, fears, and limitations, and He is abundantly able and willing to provide the wisdom you need. "It is for freedom that Christ has set us free" (Gal. 5:1). God's will is for His people to walk, not in fear and defeat, but in freedom. To do so, you must know your past and use the resources that are available to you in Christ.

THE FLORENCE FAMILY

Bob and Vera Florence were concerned. Their sons displayed some disturbing signs—especially their older son, Jeff. He was strong willed and fiercely independent. Everything had to be his own way. And he was influencing his younger brother, Lars. Having followed the parenting advice of godly teachers to no avail, the Florences sought my counsel.

Vera indicated on her counseling questionnaire that she had experiences with Ouija boards, palm reading, and other occult practices. She had come to Christ while in college and had long ago left behind all the spiritistic trappings. Bob and Vera were both deeply committed to serving Christ and were both in church leadership positions. But Jeff's issues made them wonder if they were worthy to continue as leaders.

Vera's information revealed another concern. Her mother had maintained an interest in the mystical, magical realm of the supernatural. A professing Christian, she was interested in only "white magic." Vera's mother believed the "good spirits" she contacted were from God and that they protected and helped people. It didn't require a genius to see her mother was a victim of one of Satan's most clever ploys. She did not understand that all such activities have the same source: darkness and evil.

The Florences needed to consider the spiritual ramifications of a grandparent who engaged in such activities. Jeff's negative behavior, especially the hate, rage, and profanity, suggested demonic control. Jeff had received Christ as his Savior at the age of seven. His behavior had temporarily improved, but he soon relapsed into patterns of rebellion. If he was denied some activity he really wanted to do, explosive rage seemed to always follow. "It's like something takes control of him!" Bob lamented.

Bob's description was accurate. The results that followed the aggressive practice of protective spiritual warfare indicated that powers of darkness were indeed attempting to control and dictate Jeff's behavior and responses.

The remedy was actually quite simple. God's spiritual battle plan is not complicated. It begins with direct doctrinal or prevailing prayer. The Florences learned to use their authority in Christ, coupled with their parental authority, to protect their sons. Bob and Vera followed three major steps that transformed their parenting and turned Jeff around.

First, they began in prayer to resist and forbid any claim that spiritual forces were exercising on Jeff on the basis of the ground the grandmother was giving. Two or three times each day as they went about their duties, they would invoke their protective authority through prayer.

> *In the name of my Lord Jesus Christ and by the power of His blood, I break all relationships and claims that the kingdom of darkness is focusing on Jeff because of the ground being given by his grandmother. I ask my Lord Jesus Christ to sever and break all transfer claims that the kingdom of darkness is trying to effect to gain any measure of control over Jeff, and I ask the Lord Jesus to set Jeff apart only for Himself.*

The second step was to teach Jeff to deal with his sinful nature and to resist Satan's work in his daily walk with God. (The majority of this chapter is devoted to communicating this teaching.)

The third step was to pray and establish a plan to turn the grandmother from such harmful practices. I asked them to arrange a meeting where we could all sit down together to discuss Jeff's needs. She knew of her grandson's behavior problems and had an interest in his well-being. This kind of a meeting is important. When anyone in our immediate family is living a lifestyle that gives ground to the powers of darkness, an ongoing protective and assertive renunciation of every transfer claim is necessary. Parents, grandparents, siblings, or even uncles or aunts may need to participate.*

Vera's mother agreed to meet with me on a Sunday afternoon. I kindly but firmly introduced her to what the Bible has to say about the consequences of involvement in spiritistic practices. Passages such as Deuteronomy 7:25–26 and 18:9–13 shocked her. She had no idea the Bible contained such plain words of warning. At the same time, the warnings of Exodus 20:5; 34:7; Deuteronomy 5:9 aroused her anger. She took offense at the suggestion that her interest in spiritistic practices might be causing problems in her beloved grandson's life.

I didn't press the issue. I prayed at the close of our tense discussion, asking the Lord to help Jeff's grandmother to consider the Bible's warnings about the consequences of certain sins that extend to the third and fourth generations.

Though this "truth encounter" within the family initially produced anger and raised barriers in communication, time has helped. Although they do not know whether the grandmother has renounced these practices, Bob and Vera have noted the disappearance of spiritistic literature and devices from her home. Jeff is continuing to walk in freedom. As he moves into his teen years, his parents maintain their protective stance of watchful prayer.

IT MATTERS WHO WE ARE

I'm often amazed when counselees struggle with the question "Who are you?" Many people don't really know who they are. No one has helped them face the depth of this question, which is so foundational to our spiritual and emotional well-being. Conversations in my office often go something like this:

"Who are you?"

"I'm Nancy Rogers of Kansas City."

"No, that's your name and where you live, but who are you?"

"I'm married to David Rogers; I have two children, and I teach the third grade at Parker Elementary School."

"You've given me the name of your husband, the number of children you have, and what you do, but *who are you?*"

Knowing who you are is the cornerstone to understanding the meaning of life. Parents who want the best for and from their children must instill into them biblical answers regarding their identity. Are you sure of your own worth? If so, you will be able to convey to your child his own personal worth. Each of us needs to grasp his or her value in God's sight.

A brief but profound biblical insight concerning who you are could be stated this way: "I am a person who has been created in the image and likeness of God." We ought not miss the dignity and wonder those words convey. And our children need to learn it from us.

To help facilitate a biblical understanding of personal identity, I present the following outline. Some of the outline came from my mentor and friend of many years, Dr. Victor Matthews, retired professor of theology at Grand Rapids Baptist Seminary.

WHO ARE YOU?

I. You are a person made in the image of God (Gen. 1:26–27).

  A.You have God-granted authority (Gen. 1:26).

  B.You have God-granted blessings (Gen. 1:28–30).

II. You are a person of value and dignity (Gen. 2:15–25).

  A. Our value is equal; we were all created by God as persons.

  B. Personhood communicates dignity. God always treats us as individuals. He never says, "Hey, you."

III. As persons we inherited a sinful condition from the fall of man (Gen. 3:1–13).

  A. To be sinful means you accept and believe error (Ps. 19:12; Heb. 3:10).

  B. To be sinful means you practice error (Rom. 3:9–18, 23; James 1:13–16; John 8:33–34; 1 John 3:4; James 5:20).

  C. To be sinful means you inherited a nature that wants to sin (Rom. 5:12–21; Gal. 5:17–21; Col. 3:5–8).

IV. Redeemed persons are lifted above fallen condemnation and are of great value.

  A. They are spiritual persons (John 3:6; 1 Peter 2:9–10).

  B. They are holy persons (1 Cor. 1:2; Col. 3:12; Heb. 10:10, 14).

  C. They are gifted persons (Eph. 4:7; Rom. 12:6–8).

D. They are valuable persons (Col. 3:12; Rom. 5:8; Isa. 43:1, 4).

E. They are persons loved and graced by God (John 15:9–10; 17:23).

F. They are chosen for important service (1 Peter 2:5–9).

OUR OUTWARD AND INWARD BEINGS

God values us. That's not the problem. The problem is that we value *ourselves* more than we value *Him*. Before we see how this has affected our relationship with God and how it affects our children, we need to understand how God has put us together. I follow a "tripartite" view of man's personhood. This theological view holds that each person is composed of three unique parts—body, soul, and spirit. (An alternative view argues that each person has only a body and soul, though both views agree that each person has an outward part that is visible and an inward part that is invisible.)

I believe the Bible suggests the former view is more accurate. There are numerous times when both unseen parts appear to be included when either the soul or spirit is mentioned, but biblical evidence shows a unique difference between the two. (See 1 Thess. 5:23 and Heb. 4:12.)

DOCTRINE THAT CHANGES US

At this point let's consider the doctrine of man and soteriology (how God has saved humankind, delivering us from sin's wrath through Christ). For some, this is review. For other readers, this may be new—but for all of us it is important, both for ourselves and our children.

Doctrine is important. Doctrinal truth is not just the stuff we learn in church or Sunday school. Doctrinal truth is something we are to live every day. The freedom and joy of the Christian's spiritual life are wed to this premise. Freedom demands praying and living out God's truth. Victorious freedom comes from knowing and applying doctrinal truth on a moment-by-moment basis.

THE ORIGINAL DISASTER

God's creation was perfect. Our bodies were perfectly healthy. Aging, disease, and death were not part of the original human condition. Likewise, our souls had no flaws. Our minds could grasp any and all truth. There were no such things as sadness, depression, loneliness, and fear. Human beings exercised free will. Quite simply, we were perfect.

The human spirit was the part of Adam and Eve that enabled them to commune with God. The original human couple knew God, obeyed God, and enjoyed true spiritual intimacy with Him. They were the epitome of innocence. But free will harbors the possibility of disaster. God made it so, and He presented Adam and Eve with a test. The test focused on one tree in the garden of Eden. "You are free to eat from any tree in the garden; but you must not eat from the tree of the knowledge of good and evil, for when you eat of it *you will surely die*" (Gen. 2:16–17).

Satan deceived the first innocent human creations of God, and they chose to ignore God's warning. Adam and Eve each ate the fruit of the one tree God had forbidden. It is that singular event that helps us understand the principle that underlies the delayed harvest.

Now, Adam and Eve didn't physically die that day. They continued to walk the earth for many years. Their souls didn't die either; they continued to think, feel, and make choices. So was God lying? Or was He exaggerating, just as the Serpent said? Neither one. By disobeying God and gaining a knowledge of good and evil, Adam and Eve suffered a spiritual death, the likes of which we must now all personally experience for ourselves on a daily basis.

God created us with the capacity to know Him, to obey Him, and to commune with Him in His righteousness and true holiness. But because of Adam and Eve, we have lost that connection—that right to know God personally. That is the death of which God warned His children in the garden.

NEW LIFE AND SPIRITUAL BIRTH

Thankfully, God had a plan that even Satan wasn't counting on. Jesus Christ came to earth to reverse the effects of the original disaster. He came to *redeem* us by dying on the cross. Christ's act of redemption is God's "buying us back," of paying the price for our sin. To restore us to fellowship with Him, He once again had to make us spiritually alive, to raise us back to life. Without that payment, we could not be fully restored to fellowship with Him.

Jesus said, "Flesh gives birth to flesh, but the Spirit gives birth to spirit" (John 3:6). That statement speaks to our identities. "Flesh gives birth to flesh." Our parents brought us into the world. From them we received both body and soul. We resemble them in various ways. I remember when our first granddaughter started to walk. She carried her elbows slightly behind her back. When I noticed this trait, I blurted out, "She looks just like my dad when she walks!"

We pass from generation to generation our physical and behavioral characteristics. It's even true of our personalities. We can't help but give to our kids part of what makes us who we are. Our emotional responses, attitudes, quirks of personality—even our many *sinful* appetites and habits—are part of what we inherit from Mom and Dad. "Flesh gives birth to flesh ..."

The second part of John 3:6 is just as important as the first. "Spirit gives birth to spirit." God's plan to redeem us required a new birth so we could have new life. Our spirits, now dead, come to life the moment we receive Jesus Christ as our Savior. A spiritual rebirth takes place, and the Holy Spirit permanently unites with our spirits.

This spiritual rebirth is due to nothing other than the grace of God. Ephesians 4:24 (NKJV) says the rebirth results in a "new man which was created according to God, in true righteousness and holiness." Although God continues to perfect our reborn human spirits in knowledge and understanding, our spirits are not only alive, but also completely holy in His eyes. Since the Holy Spirit now lives in us, God views our spirits as perfect.

Even though our spirits have been redeemed, however, our souls still need much work. Even after our spiritual regeneration, our mind, our will, and our emotions must go through a lifetime process of growth. God sanctifies us, a process whereby He makes us more and more like Jesus. We daily learn to yield control of our thoughts, feelings, and actions to the Holy Spirit. This process will continue until the Lord returns or until our death. At that very moment the process will be complete. But until then, each believer lives with a spirit that sometimes feels crippled by a corrupted soul.

The body of the believer will eventually enter an environment of total righteousness and holiness in God's presence. This does not happen until, at our Lord's return, a resurrection takes place. Each believer will live forever in a brand-new, imperishable, and perfect body, just as the apostle Paul described in Philippians 3:20–21.

The following outlines show the outcome of our lives after the fall and after the redemption God provided through Jesus Christ.

Humanity after the Fall

I. Consequences on the body

   A. Receives the judgment sentence of eventual physical death with all death's consequent expressions

   B. Susceptible to pain, toil, disease, and various afflictions and sufferings

   C. Able to use all of its senses and capacities to serve self, sin, and Satan

   D. Doomed to eventually die, decay, and return to the physical elements of its creation

II. Consequences on the soul and spirit

   A. The soul maintains a corrupted personality in identity with God; it seems to have assumed the internal actions and decisions God originally assigned to the spirit.

     1. Intellect: able to receive, use, and evaluate knowledge to do one's own will and to decide one's own religion; cannot know or please God

     2. Will: now corrupted to serve the interests, appetites, and desires of self, sin, and Satan; unable to choose or will to do God's will; is held in the bondage of Satan's deceptions

     3. Emotions: now corrupted to experience feelings of anger, hate, fear, etc., that flow from self, sin, and Satan's deceptive rule

   B. The spirit died immediately at the fall and is no longer able to function.

     1. No capacity to know God, obey Him, or commune with Him in a pleasing manner

   2. Unable to worship God in spirit and truth

   3. Correct spiritual understanding of God no longer possible unless the spirit is restored to life

REDEMPTION: A NEW BIRTH

I. Consequences on the body

  A. New features

    1. Receives the first breath of the quickening life of the Holy Spirit's presence as a deposit guaranteeing its eventual glorification (Eph. 1:14)

    2. Able to function in a manner that serves and pleases God (Rom. 6:14)

    3. Is made a "holy" body by the saving work of grace and the indwelling presence of the Holy Spirit (Rom. 12:1–2)

  B. Features remaining from the fall

    1. Appetites and desires that were corrupted by the fall

    2. Pain, disease, weakness, and defects that will culminate in physical death

    3. Remains a focus point the "flesh" will use to create desire for sinful acts and thoughts

II. Consequences on the soul and spirit

  A. The soul can renew a personal relationship with God in a way that pleases Him, though a fallen nature can interrupt this fellowship.

    1. New features

      a. An intellect renewed by the Holy Spirit's work to receive, evaluate, and use knowledge of truth to serve and glorify God

      b. A will with renewed capacities under the Holy Spirit's control to choose and act in ways that will please and glorify God

  c. Emotions with the renewed capacity to receive and live out the fruit of the Spirit

 2. Features remaining from the fall

  a. An intellect with fallen desires still present, which may cause the mind to make choices to please the sinful appetites of the flesh rather than God

  b. A will that can decide to give in to the corrupt and sinful desires of the flesh

  c. Emotions that still have capacities to feel and experience the depraved desires inherited from the fall

  d. A soul still subject to making fleshly choices that produce a chastened, lukewarm Christian life

B. The spirit is restored to life, righteousness, and true holiness by the regenerating, indwelling work of the Holy Spirit.

 1. Able to be the conduit for the Holy Spirit to bring renewing life and control to the wholeness of the redeemed person's mind, will, and emotions

 2. Through the Holy Spirit, able to make righteous choices to obey and serve God in His will and plan

 3. Through the Holy Spirit, able to love God and to fulfill his desire to worship and know God

FACING OUR ENEMY

Many Christians blame all their problems on the Devil. It is true, some of our struggles do come from our spiritual Enemy. But is it right to put off all responsibility for our depravity?

James, the leader of the church in Jerusalem and our Lord's half brother, wrote a letter to some of his Jewish converts. The flames of spiritual revival had over the years diminished. It was challenging to live in a pagan world as a follower of Jesus, so James addressed that very issue. The apostle at one point compared a false wisdom that produces "bitter envy and selfish ambition" with true wisdom from heaven that is "pure ... peace-loving, considerate, submissive, full of mercy and good fruit" (see James 3:13–17).

James taught that false wisdom comes from one of three sources: the world (earthly), fleshly appetites (sensual), or the Devil or one of his demons (v. 15). The apostle presented these three enemies in the order in which believers need to deal with them, but we'll deal with the second one first.

The Sinful Nature. Within each of us there resides a sinful nature, what some Bible translations refer to as "the flesh." It is our bent toward evil that began when Adam and Eve disobeyed God. That sinful nature has been passed to us over the generations and is the source of the desires that battle within us. We must learn to control and weaken its power.

The World. Our external enemy, "the world," refers to the system of corrupt ethics, rationalization, and values in which we live, work, and play. It continually seeks to befriend us (James 4:4), tempting us to compromise our spiritual values. To choose the world is to become an enemy of God. James warns believers that they have the capacity to be God's enemy for at least a season of time.

The Devil. The final enemy is supernatural evil (James 4:7–10). God commands believers to "resist the devil." Scriptural imperatives such as "submit to God," "draw near to God," and "humble yourselves in the sight of the Lord" make clear that when we are in proper relationship with Him, our problems with evil will be minimal.

James called for a clean break with sin. "Wash your hands, you sinners, and purify your hearts, you double-minded. Grieve, mourn and wail! Change your laughter to mourning and your joy to gloom" (4:8–9). A word of caution here: The Lord is not against joyful celebration. James's point was to deal with unresolved sin *before* we celebrate our victories. He told us to let go of the sins we want to keep part of our lives. When a believer fails to renounce sin's rule, the Devil will soon have that person in his destructive grip.

The Devil can use anything to sabotage our walk with God. He can use success, money, entertainment, and even religion to turn us from God toward our own self-advancement. We have the ability and tendency to turn even good things into idols. It is a parent's responsibility to keep him- or herself from worshipping an "idol" and to help his or her child to recognize when something is becoming too important in that child's life. It may be hard for our children to hear, but sometimes we may need to say, "You know, son, it appears to me that your devotion to your sports (or music, girlfriend, boyfriend, etc.) is becoming an idol and overshadowing everything else in your life." We need to help them to recognize how the Adversary uses such things to get hold of their lives.

OUTLINES ON OUR SPIRITUAL ENEMIES

The final outlines on our spiritual enemies should be studied carefully. The defeat of God's plan for believers to walk in freedom is a result of our own failure to resist the evil spiritual influences in our lives. Parents who desire to walk in freedom and to teach their children to do so should prayerfully study these outlines.

REDEEMED PERSONS FACING THEIR ENEMY, THE WORLD

I. The nature of the enemy

   A. The world is an external enemy that puts pressure on the believer to conform to its value system.

      1. It is a philosophy. *Aior*, one Greek word for *world*, appears more than forty times in most English translations of the New Testament. This word refers to the attitude, teaching, or prevailing philosophy of the culture in which a believer lives (Rom. 12:1–3; 2 Cor. 4:4).

      2. It is an organized system. The Greek word *kosmos* is translated *world* in most English translations more than 160 times. This word focuses on the organized structure and system of function in the world (James 4:4–6; 1 John 2:15–17).

   B. The world is the enemy of God and the enemy of truth and righteousness. Satan is called the world's god, and friendship with it aligns one as God's enemy (2 Cor. 4:4; James 4:4–6).

II. How the world pressures me to conform to its organized value system

   A. It is the "marketing department" of the appetites (1 John 2:16).

1. The world offers in attractive packages what its citizens' fallen natures desire.

2. Advertising, media presentations, and social programs offer fleshly appeal to attract attention and give the flesh what it wants.

B. It is the "marketing department" for the clever and deceptive lies of Satan and his kingdom. As the "god of this age," Satan introduces his deceptive rule over the nations (2 Cor. 4:4; Eph. 2:1–2).

C. It pressures believers through its many organized and philosophical expressions to conform to its value system.

1. The organized worlds of politics, education, finance, taxation, and religion, for example, all pressure us to conform.

2. The sensual appeal of the philosophical worlds of entertainment, music, fashion, literature, and advertising add to the world's pressure to conform.

III. God's resources for overcoming the pressures and temptations of the world's system

A. The truth embodied in the gospel and the Christian faith equips believers to evaluate the world's fare (1 John 5:1–5).

B. Knowledge of biblical ways to overcome the world's fleshly temptations will enable believers to resist the world's fleshly offerings (Gal. 5:16-25).

C. Biblical knowledge of the believer's weapons of warfare against Satan's deceptive and threatening ways will equip believers to resist and overcome Satan's worldly tactics (James 4:7–10).

Redeemed Persons Facing Satan's Kingdom

I. Satan's kingdom—internal and external

  A. External significance of the kingdom

    1. Satan is called the god of this age or world (2 Cor. 4:4). Satan's chief place of influence and rule is over the world. He and his wicked spirits work to control both the philosophy and organized structure of the world system.

    2. Satan is not omnipresent like God, though he functions with a diverse, organized kingdom of spirit beings who can communicate with him instantaneously from any geographic location in the world.

    3. Satan tries to force his evil plans and God-rejecting will on nonbelievers by his control over them (Eph. 2:1–3).

    4. Satan tries to defeat believers by having his demonic host directly attack them or use the world's organized structure to hinder them (Eph. 6:10–13).

  B. Internal significance of the kingdom

    1. As personal spirit beings, Satan and his host of fallen angels are able to project thoughts, emotions, and a rebellious attitude into the mind, will, emotions, and body of a believer. With subtle, deceptive cleverness, internalized rule is attempted.

    2. It is often difficult for believers to discern the difference between their own thoughts, emotions, and will from those of satanic origin (Matt. 16:21–23).

    3. If ground is given to the kingdom of darkness by a believer, internal affliction, rule, and control

will be experienced by that believer (Eph. 4:25–28; 2 Tim. 2:26).

II. An evil, supernatural kingdom
  A. It is a kingdom ruled and headed by Satan.
    1. Satan is one of the most powerful of all God's created beings (Jude v. 9).
    2. Satan is a created angelic being who rebelled against God and led one-third of the created angels to follow him in rebellion (Rev. 12:4).
  B. It is a kingdom organized and structured to defeat believers in their assigned task to evangelize the world and glorify God in the world (Eph. 6:10–12).
  C. Satan's kingdom is a powerful kingdom, though infinitely inferior to God's and will ultimately be judged by consignment to the lake of fire (Matt. 25:41; Rev. 20:10).

III. How Satan's kingdom tempts believers to do evil
  A. He tempts believers to deceive and to be deceived (John 8:44; Acts 5:1–4).
  B. He tempts believers to be fearful (1 Peter 5:8–9).
  C. He tempts believers to question God's Word, God's attributes, and God's will (Gen. 3:1–6).
  D. He accuses believers and attempts to torment them with false guilt (Rev. 12:10–12).
  E. He tempts us to destroy our lives or to take our lives by suicide (Heb. 2:14–15; John 8:43–45).
  F. He tempts believers to excuse their fleshly sins to take advantage of them (Eph. 4:17–29).
  G. He seeks to get us to justify our lack of forgiveness, to manipulate us into his control.
    1. Toward others (Matt. 18:21–35)

    2. Toward self (John 21:15–19; cf. Luke 22:31–37)

H. He tempts believers to pride (1 Tim. 3:6–7).

    1. To use God's power for personal gain (Luke 4:1–4)

    2. To worship Satan and to desire his power (Luke 4:5–8)

    3. To test God's Word and His promises (Luke 4:9–13)

IV. Resources for believers to defeat Satan and walk in freedom from Satan's rule

  A. God has provided four citadels that make a believer invincible over Satan's kingdom in the doing of God's will (Eph. 6:10–20).

    1. The believer's union with Jesus Christ in all of His person and work (Eph. 6:10a) (The phrase "be strong in the Lord" or its equivalent is used more than forty times in Ephesians.)

      a. In His name (Acts 9:15; Col. 3:17; Rev. 3:12)

      b. In His incarnation (Col. 1:22; 2:9–10)

      c. In His cross (Gal. 2:20; Heb. 2:14–15)

      d. In His resurrection (Eph. 2:6; John 14:19)

      e. In His ascension (Eph. 1:20–23; 2:6–7)

      f. In His glorification (Eph. 2:6; Rom. 8:30)

      g. In His return (Col. 3:4; 1 Thess. 4:15–18)

    2. The person and work of the Holy Spirit (Eph. 6:10b) We must keep the focus on His ministries to believers.

      a. Convicting ministry (John 16:7–11)

      b. Indwelling ministry (Rom. 8:9)

      c. Sealing ministry (Eph. 1:13–14)

      d. Baptizing ministry (1 Cor. 12:13)

      e. Quickening ministry (Rom. 8:9–11)

      f. Interceding ministry (Rom. 8:26–27)

g. Filling ministry (Eph. 5:17–18)

3. The whole armor of God (Eph. 6:11–17)
   a. Belt of truth (Eph. 6:14a)
   b. Breastplate of righteousness (Eph. 6:14b)
   c. Shoes of peace (Eph. 6:15)
   d. Shield of faith (Eph. 6:16)
   e. Helmet of salvation (Eph. 6:17a)
   f. Sword of the Spirit (Eph. 6:17b)

4. The "allness" of prayer (Eph. 6:18–20)
   a. The paraclete of prayer (in the Spirit)
   b. The persistence of prayer (on all occasions)
   c. The parameters of prayer (with all kinds of prayers)
   d. The protection of prayer (be alert)
   e. The panorama of prayer (for all the saints)
   f. The projection of prayer (for me) (Paul wanted prepared, penetrating, courageous words to share.)

B. To walk in freedom requires the aggressive application of the provided victory and not passive assumption. (Note the frequent imperatives in Ephesians 6.)

WE CHRISTIAN PARENTS
MUST LEARN HOW TO
HANDLE OUR OWN
SINFUL NATURES AS
WELL AS TEACH OUR
CHILDREN HOW TO DEAL
WITH THEIRS.

7

Learning to Walk in Freedom

Whon he was ten years old, Link found his father's pornographic magazines. The magazines weren't hidden well, and Link began to look at the photographs inside. Later, as a single man in his late twenties, he came to see me and described what he called "bondage." The bondage involved sexual fantasies and compulsive masturbation. Link had read my book *The Adversary* and regarded me as his best hope. He began our meeting with a description of what a horrible person he was. I interrupted him.

"Link, are you a Christian believer?"

"Yes, I *think* I am, but sometimes I wonder! I can't see how a Christian could do the things I do."

Link told me his story of how he had come to trust Jesus Christ as his Savior at a Billy Graham crusade. His new faith initially brought him peace and an inward release from the guilt and self-hatred that had plagued him all of his life.

Tears coursed down Link's face as he recalled his conversion. "I'll never forget it. I started to pray with my counselor, and as I asked Jesus to come into my life and cleanse me from my sins, something wonderful happened. I'd been weeping over my guilt and sinfulness, but all of a sudden, I realized my tears had changed. I was now crying out of sheer joy and gratitude. The weight of my sins lifted away, and a sense of inner cleanness overwhelmed me.

"But that's why I feel so bad now. It was so great for several weeks, but when I began to slip back into some of my old sins again, everything began to change. I think I feel more guilt and defeat now than I did before Jesus saved me."

Link's recurring defeats involved sexual sins. When he saw an attractive woman on the street, it often triggered a sexual fantasy. He would return home, mentally undress the woman, and imagine engaging with her in sexual activity, which in his make-believe world she welcomed and enjoyed. After he masturbated, Link loathed himself. Guilt devastated him, and the defeat felt like a shroud of death.

Link diagnosed his own problem. "I must have a demon of lust controlling me.... I hate it so much, but I'm so helpless. I get drawn into it before I know what I'm doing. Will you help me get free from this wicked demon? Please!"

DEALING WITH OUR FLESH

Link's story is typical of people with besetting sins that torment them. His story underscores how parents can unintentionally, yet adversely, influence their children. As an adult, Link recognized his need to accept responsibility for his actions.

The selfish pursuit of personal desires begins early in life. Our twin grandchildren, Cambria and Andrew, were playing at our home during a visit when they were only about a year old. Cambria was slightly ahead of Andrew in motor skills, and she would often hand him toys she knew he liked.

What a sweet picture of innocence it was. Later, however, Andrew took something from Cambria, and I saw a different side of my granddaughter. She watched him struggle to stand, wobbling back and forth. And just when he seemed to have gained his balance, Cambria reached over and gave her brother a little push on the shoulder. Andrew tumbled to the floor in a twisted mass of arms and legs, and my illusion of her innocence collapsed along with him. She stood there quite pleased with herself, while Andrew whimpered in complaint.

Our sinful nature reveals itself early in childhood. We Christian parents must learn how to handle our own sinful natures as well as teach our children how to deal with theirs. We can neither model nor teach our children with confidence if we continually yield to our sinful nature. Our frequent sins range from anger, jealousy, and self-promotion to sexual sins. They keep us from developing a close relationship with God and effective leadership of our children. And the source of most of it is our own sinful nature.

THE FLESH AND DEPRAVITY

Do you know what is meant by *total depravity?* It's probably a term you don't hear very often. Total depravity is the biblical teaching that the corruption of Adam's fall extends to every part of a person. Consequently, there is nothing in us that can make us worthy in the presence of a holy God. We may not always behave as badly as we can, but even the noblest of our actions has at its core depraved motives and methods. Most of us can theoretically acknowledge the total depravity of *other* people. But what about when we have to acknowledge our own depravity? Or that of our precious and "perfect" children? That is a far more difficult proposition!

Depravity is an internal problem that is woven into the very nature of every person. David wrote in Psalm 51:5 that our sinful nature didn't begin at birth, but at the moment of conception. Our sin nature runs deep indeed.

Theologians and Bible translators have struggled to find the proper words to describe this basic sin problem. In the King James Version, Galatians 5:16 uses the word "flesh" to describe our struggle with sin. "Walk in the Spirit, and ye shall not fulfill the lust of the flesh." The New International Version instead uses the phrase "sinful nature" to show that this is a struggle that we all deal with during our time on earth. "So I say, live by the Spirit, and you will not gratify the desires of the sinful nature."

"Lust of the flesh" and "desires of the sinful nature" both describe the temptation to sin that we all face, regardless of age. Our children need parents to provide biblical insight to overcome this basic desire to act out their sinful nature. We must not blame all our temptations on the Devil; that's an incomplete picture. At the core of the problem is an internal, depraved human condition.

Understanding this basic doctrine is foundational to our comprehension of the struggle with sin, yet most believers don't know how to deal with this most basic issue.

THE GREAT WRESTLING MATCH

We can thank Adam for our sinful natures. That's where it began. And it doesn't end after we trust Christ and experience the new birth. Our sinful desires remain totally wicked and depraved. We can never reform, improve, or remove them, because they are part of our spiritual genetics. We overcome them only through the consistent application to our lives of Christ's resurrection power. But how do we do that? The apostle Paul, in two different letters to believers in what is now Turkey, described both the problem and the solution.

"The acts of the sinful nature are obvious: sexual immorality, impurity and debauchery; idolatry and witchcraft; hatred, discord, jealousy, fits of rage, selfish ambitions, dissensions, factions and envy; drunkenness, orgies, and the like" (Gal. 5:19–21).

> Put to death, therefore, whatever belongs to your earthly nature: sexual immorality, impurity, lust, evil desires and greed, which is idolatry. Because of these, the wrath of God is coming. You used to walk in these ways, in the life you once lived. But now you must rid yourselves of all such things as these: anger, rage, malice, slander, and filthy language from your lips. Do not lie to each other. (Col. 3:5–9)

Paul said to believers, "You *can* wrestle our sinful nature and *win!* The power is available!"

THE POWER TO OVERCOME TEMPTATIONS

The two passages you just read are remarkably similar. Paul described in both of them the fleshly sins believers are to overcome. Every believer faces temptations remarkably similar to those of everyone else in the world. Because of our "flesh," we must deal with desires and temptations that are just like the ones we faced before our new birth. The difference is that we don't have to let those temptations get the upper hand and win the wrestling match. Christ's salvation has provided us with every resource we need so as to "not fulfill the lust of the flesh" (Gal. 5:16 NKJV). We can defeat temptations.

I remember how liberating it was for Link when the Holy Spirit enabled him to understand this truth. He thought the new birth would free him from the drives that had controlled him since his childhood. When the old desires reemerged after his conversion, he was devastated with false guilt. He equated the temptation itself with sin. And Satan, the Accuser, used Link's ignorance to lead him into sin: "You've already fantasized, so you might as well go ahead and act out! Since you're guilty anyway, you might as well enjoy it." Link would eventually give in to the constant barrage of inner accusations. Remorse and guilt inevitably followed.

What had Link failed to recognize? Temptation is not sin. I instructed him to memorize Hebrews 4:14–15:

> Therefore, since we have a great high priest who has gone through the heavens, Jesus the Son of God, let us hold firmly to the faith we profess. For we do not have a high priest who is unable to sympathize with our weaknesses, but we have one who has been tempted in every way, just as we are—yet was without sin.

Even our Lord Jesus Christ experienced temptation. He understands the appeal it holds. The difference is, He never gave in. He is now qualified and willing to help us live above our temptations and desires.

HOW TO OVERCOME YOUR SINFUL DESIRES

Temptation is part of our lives as believers, but we need not give in to it. Here's what to do the next time your sinful nature challenges you to a wrestling match.

RECALL THE THREE ABSOLUTE TRUTHS ON WHICH FREEDOM IS BASED

An absolute is a truth that stands alone. It is an indisputable fact because God Himself has made it true. Acting on the three absolutes found in Colossians 3 will enable us to walk in freedom from fleshly rule.

1. Every believer has resurrection life (Col. 3:1–2). This resurrection with Christ occurred even before we put our faith in Him as our personal Lord and Savior. It happened during the historic event itself. Christ's resurrection was our resurrection, according to the apostle Paul. The mighty power that raised the Lord Jesus Christ from the grave dwells in each believer. Since resurrection life dwells in us, we are to set our hearts and minds on heavenly things.

2. Every believer has union with Christ in His death. At the cross, every believer died, even before he or she believed. Christ's death was our death. Our union with Christ is what frees us from the penalty of sin and the power of sin to hold us in bondage. As believers, our union with Christ is safe and secure. "Your life is now hidden with Christ in God" (Col. 3:3).

3. Every believer has union with Christ in His second coming (Col. 3:4). This absolute hasn't happened yet, but it is just as certain as the first two, which are based on historical events. Every believer will appear with Christ in the glory of His second coming.

APPLY YOUR FREEDOM BIBLICALLY

Doctrinal truth based on the absolutes of God is not meant to be passively accepted. These truths are to be lived out in daily life.

Walk in honest admission and confession (Col. 3:5–10). The word *therefore* in verse 5 ("Put to death, therefore …") points us back to the three absolutes of grace mentioned above. Believers can walk in freedom from the rule of this long list of sins when we apply these three absolutes.

According to Galatians 5:19, "The acts of the sinful nature are obvious." To whom are these acts of the flesh obvious? They are obvious to God and to our Lord Jesus Christ. God knows these desires flow to us from our fallen condition, and He wants us to know it too. Understanding this truth is crucial to freedom. We must not expect more of ourselves than what God has presently provided for. This truth can liberate us from much false guilt.

Walk in the truth of your death with Christ. Four key New Testament texts declare the believer's death with Christ or command that we act as those who are dead to our sinful nature: Romans 6:11; Galatians 5:24; Colossians 3:3, 5. Each text speaks to the necessity of recognizing how God has equipped the believer to overcome the desires of the flesh by the cross of Christ.

Walk in the control of the Holy Spirit (Gal. 5:16, 18, 22–23, 25). When the Holy Spirit controls the believer, a much different life is produced than what the fleshly, earthly nature can produce. We need to remember our identity as Christ's followers. According to Colossians 3:12, we are "God's chosen people, holy and dearly loved."

God chose us to be the conduits through which His message of love and grace would flow to the world. God calls us holy, even though we may not feel at times we are living in a holy way. Justification has made every believer holy in God's sight. The very righteousness of Jesus Christ has been credited to each believer in his or her standing before God. And though we may struggle with sins, we are greatly loved. The Lord is on your side. He is not angry and displeased with you because of your failures. He loves you.

According to Colossians 3:12, we should "clothe ourselves with compassion, kindness, humility, gentleness and patience." Well, who was compassionate, kind, humble, gentle, and patient? Jesus! Be like Jesus! We can be more and more like Jesus as we allow the power that raised Jesus Christ from the dead to control our minds, wills, emotions, and bodies. The Holy Spirit will shape us more and more to look and act like Jesus. That is His work. He is the one who applies Christ's resurrection life to our individual experiences.

Once again, here are three major steps for overcoming the flesh:

1. Acknowledge that Christ has set you free to choose *not* to sin. After all, you now possess within you the resurrection life and power of Christ (Col. 3:1–2). Consequently, you are now free from both the penalty and the power of sin.

2. Engage in daily "spiritual conditioning." Keep short accounts with God, confessing your sins (1 John 1:9). Ask the Lord to show you attitudes, actions, and habits of which you need to rid yourself (Col. 3:5–10). Then daily yield yourself in prayer to the empowerment and direction of the Holy Spirit. In short, surrender, and allow the Holy Spirit to *lead you*, which means literally, to "walk around with you" (Gal. 5:16, 18).

3. Pray daily. Ask the Lord Jesus Christ to clothe you with His compassion, kindness, humility, gentleness, and patience (Col. 3:12).

PRAYERS THAT WORK

The three steps above can be applied through prayer and by following Christ. Let's consider each step in practical terms.

First, when a temptation or desire initially presents itself, we must be diligent to address our need to the Lord and to pray about that specific temptation. Pray in this manner:

> *Lord Jesus Christ, my old fleshly nature is tempting me to* _____ *[name the temptation], and I know that if left to itself, it is wicked enough to cause me to sin against You.*

This kind of frankness in prayer is liberating. It identifies your need. Don't try to convince yourself that your flesh isn't as bad as God says it is. Honest assessment is key to defeating temptation.

Second, act on the truth that you have died with Christ. Acknowledge that you are "dead to sin but alive to God in Christ Jesus" (Rom. 6:11). Express your freedom to overcome sin with a prayer like this:

> *Lord Jesus Christ, I affirm that through the*
> *work of Your cross I am dead with You to the rule*
> *and control of my flesh and its desire to _____ [name*
> *the sin]."*

Freedom from sin's control does not mean freedom from temptation. Jesus told us temptation is a "given" in our earthly life. Only after we go to be with our Lord will temptation be a thing of the past. Perhaps that is why the Lord doesn't eradicate our sinful natures in this life: Our struggle with temptation keeps us close to the cross and dependent on Christ's power.

Third, yield to the Holy Spirit's control. The Holy Spirit doesn't force His way on us. God respects us too much for that. He waits for us to ask the Holy Spirit to do what He is eager to accomplish. We should in prayer say this to Him:

> *Blessed Holy Spirit, I ask You now to replace*
> *this fleshly desire that is tempting me to _____*
> *[name the desire] with the fruit of Your control.*
> *Put within my mind, will, emotions, and body Your*
> *love, joy, peace, patience, and all the virtues that*
> *my Lord Jesus Christ enables me to live out for His*
> *glory."*

Every temptation we face requires this application of truth every time we feel its pressure. We should apply all three steps moment by moment as we walk through each day.

FOLLOWING THE PLAN

After our second meeting together, Link could accurately and confidently repeat these three steps back to me. I was certain he would do well in overcoming his temptation. The actual outcome disappointed me.

Link called me a few days later. He sounded desperate. "Oh, Pastor Bubeck! You must help me get rid of this demon of lust. I just failed again, and I'm so ashamed."

"Link, what are the three biblical steps to overcoming your flesh?" I interrupted his lament by forcing him to consider where he lost the battle. Silence. I waited.

"I can't remember," Link admitted. "This demon of lust has me too upset."

"Link," I responded, "if you won't use the biblical steps to victory that the Lord has provided, I can't help you."

He apologized, and I patiently once again taught him the three steps. Then I got in his face. "Link, don't bother to call me again or ask for any appointment if you can't recite these steps to me. I won't talk to you or see you until you convince me you are using this biblical prescription."

After prayer, we concluded the call. Link was in church on Sunday, but he didn't greet me at the door. He was in the midweek prayer service but wouldn't talk to me. I wondered if I'd been too tough on him. Several more days passed before he eventually called back. I asked, "Link, what are the three biblical steps God has given us to overcome our flesh?"

His response was quick and decisive. "Walk in honesty! Walk in death! And walk in the Spirit!"

I was ecstatic! After I congratulated him, he responded, "That really works, doesn't it?"

And *why* does it work? It works because it is the application of biblical truth. Many people, however, are unwilling to learn and apply something as simple as these three principles.

Those who do so discover that the use of God's truth ensures one's freedom.

TEACHING THE PLAN TO OUR CHILDREN

As an adult, Link learned how to deal with his enemy. How much better it is to prepare our young children to deal with the Adversary. Unfortunately, well-meaning Christian parents fall into a dangerous trap when they try to help their children to simply *manage* instead of to *defeat* their sinful nature.

Anger, jealousy, quarreling, and divisiveness are common fleshly sins all children experience. If they know the Lord Jesus, we should teach them about their spiritual resources. Discipline certainly has its place. Children need to learn that these sins are unacceptable to us and to God. Wise parents, however, will begin to train children in the biblical principles that enable them to defeat temptation. Begin at an early age. It requires patience, persistence, and loving repetition, but the rewards will amaze you.

Remember Suzy in chapter 3? At five years old she experienced out-of-control rages caused by a generational transfer problem. Her aging grandfather had lived a life of cruel, drunken rages, often abusing his son, Jim. Only as Jim and his wife practiced protective warfare prayer over their daughter were they able to eliminate the demonic control from Suzy's life.

Suzy's quick temper wasn't a problem with demonization, however. It was a problem with a sinful nature. Suzy had received the Lord Jesus Christ when she was four. After Suzy's parents had broken the demonic activity, they began patiently to teach her how to put off her sinful anger. It amazed us to see Suzy quickly understand. Her keen mind and spiritual sensitivity helped her to deal with her anger problem.

She understood well the biblical principles of being dead with Christ and controlled by the Spirit. Her mother would hear her say, "I'm dead with Jesus to the control of anger. I ask the Holy Spirit to put love and joy and peace inside my heart." Suzy's behavior took a radical turn. Her anger came under control.

Suzy is now ten years old. It has required patient teaching and repetition by her godly parents, but she is learning to walk in her freedom. What discipline and reasoning couldn't do, grace and truth are accomplishing.

GUIDELINES FOR TEACHING VICTORY TO CHILDREN

Teaching your child the biblical principles of this chapter is vital. If your child knows Jesus as his or her Savior, it is not too early to start. Here are several guidelines to remember as you teach the three steps to freedom.

- Be sure that you, as a Christian parent, understand and practice your own freedom from the rule of the sinful nature.
- Make sure that your child has made a personal decision to trust Jesus Christ as Lord and Savior.
- Watch for the major "besetting" sin evident in each child's life. (Anger, lying, greed, and jealousy are common to children.) Arrange a time to talk about the problem and to teach in an age-appropriate manner the three steps to freedom.
- Pray for the Lord to help the child apply His freedom.
- Be prepared to repeat the lesson as the child grows and other sins appear.
- When you take note of victory over the sinful nature, commend your child.
- Avoid shaming the child or relying on discipline to

transform the fleshly nature. Depend on the application of spiritual truth to effect change.

❑ Watch for evidence of demonic attempts to rule your child. Consistently practice aggressive spiritual warfare protection over your children.

8

Preventing Demonic Harassment

To overcome the Adversary in our homes requires us to stay confident and able to ward off the attacks our children may face. We must not only know what to do for our children but stay strong ourselves. We saw in the previous chapter how to strengthen ourselves and our children against our sinful natures. We must now consider what happens if we let sin progress in our lives or in the lives of our children.

Indulgence in sin can expose us and our family to demonic harassment. Such was the case with Link. He returned to my office in jubilation after winning some victories but feeling intense frustration when at other times he yielded to temptation.

"Pastor, I don't want to be disrespectful of your efforts to help me," he said during our meeting, "but I still think a demon of lust is trying to rule and torment me. I'm using my victory over my flesh on a regular basis now. It has wonderfully helped me, but sometimes I seem to hear voices in my mind that laugh at me. Then the temptation starts all over again, and I wonder about my sanity."

Link's query was obviously sincere. He was still hurting. I was not surprised. His mention of his father's use of pornography presented the possibility of a generational transfer problem. The other red flag suggesting demonic harassment related to the lengthy period that Link had willfully practiced his fleshly sin of perverted sexual lust. He would need to deal with the realm of unclean spirits before his freedom would be complete.

Experience and biblical common sense had taught me that progress against the kingdom of darkness is impossible if fleshly sin is ongoing. Ephesians 4 proved to be eye opening for Link. He came to understand that excusing fleshly sins leads to deeper problems with sin.

NO EXCUSES FOR SINS OF THE FLESH

We as parents must respond promptly to sins we observe in ourselves and in our children. If we love them, we want to keep them from sliding into deeper problems, including demonic harassment. To do this, we need to help our children face their own fleshly attitudes or actions. The Scriptures warn us against excusing sin in our lives. Consider the warnings in Ephesians 4:17–18 about treating sin with indifference. It was a passage Link and I carefully examined.

> So I tell you this, and insist on it in the Lord, that you must no longer live as the Gentiles do, in the futility of their thinking. They are darkened in their understanding and separated from the life of God because of the ignorance that is in them due to the hardening of their hearts.

Those words convey urgency. Believers are not to live like nonbelievers. Nonbelievers suffer from a futile thought process that is darkened to the truth. That's scary. This conveys the truth of Ephesians 2:1–3, which describes the Prince of Darkness as "the ruler of the kingdom of the air, the spirit who is now at work in those who are disobedient." What rules non-Christians? Their appetites and the rule of Satan's kingdom. And most don't even realize it.

Paul next explained the principle of increasing oppression: "Having lost all sensitivity, they have given themselves over to sensuality so as to indulge in every kind of impurity, with a continual lust for more" (Eph. 4:19). The practice of fleshly sins always leads into more and more oppression. "That's certainly the way it is with me," Link confessed.

The sins we indulge inevitably get worse. It's like an addiction: The more we try it, the more we want it. The law of diminishing returns sets in, and it takes more to satisfy us. It matters little whether one is a believer or a nonbeliever. The more we indulge the appetites of the flesh, the more intense our desires become, and we progress into other, even deeper sins.

Indulgence of the "old self" has no place in a Christian's life. "Surely you heard of him and were taught in him in accordance with the truth that is in Jesus. You were taught, with regard to your former way of life, to put off your old self, which is being corrupted by its deceitful desires" (Eph. 4:21–22).

The truth that is in Jesus should instruct our lives. Devotion to His teaching and the Holy Spirit's guidance will lead us to put off the rule and control of fleshly desires. Freedom from desire does not happen simply because one received salvation. It requires instruction and an active "putting off." This takes place as we follow the first two steps to victory over the flesh, just as learned in the previous chapter.

To put off the desires of the old self requires an honest confession and recognition that we are "dead with Christ" to sin. We must acknowledge our fleshly desire and admit its potential to lead us into sin. A simple and helpful prayer is "Lord Jesus, my fleshly nature is at it again, and I know that it's wicked enough to lead me into sin if left to itself." Another prayer to recite is "Lord Jesus, I affirm that because of Your sacrificial death on the cross, I am dead to the rule and control of this fleshly desire."

Victory requires a third step—a renewed mind. Paul wrote, "Be made new in the attitude of your minds; and ... put on the new self, created to be like God in true righteousness and holiness" (Eph. 4:23–24).

How can a believer renew his mind? He can reach out at the moment of temptation and ask the Holy Spirit to do what He has promised to do. Ask Him to control your attitudes (step three mentioned in the previous chapter). A sample prayer (like the one Link said) goes like this: "I now ask the Holy Spirit to remove and replace this fleshly desire with the fruit of His control. Put within me Your love, joy, peace, patience, and all I need to respond to this temptation as my Savior would."

As believers practice these simple applications of truth, they will experience freedom from the rule of the flesh. Link's problem, however, did not fully abate as he employed these principles. Paul tells us why in verses 25–27: "Therefore each of you must put off falsehood and speak truthfully to his neighbor, for we are all members of one body. 'In your anger do not sin': Do not let the sun go down while you are still angry, and do not give the devil a foothold."

Both lying and anger are expressions of our sinful natures. (See Col. 3:9; Gal. 5:19–21.) We must put off lying. We must not hold on to and justify anger when it originates in our flesh. We must not excuse it with faulty words such as "I have good reason to be angry. Did you see what that person did to me?" Many of us struggle either with temptations to deceive or to display inappropriate anger. Sometimes both temptations plague us. We must not excuse them as "lesser sins" or say, "That's just the way I am."

When we fail to deal with each sin as it rears its ugly head and when we do not seek victory, we give the Devil a "foothold" (Eph. 4:27). Footholds become strongholds that facilitate the rule of the powers of darkness. A demon can use a foothold as a point of rule and control in the area where we give ground. Link's problem had become more than fleshly rule; the laughter he heard in his mind indicated the existence of a stronghold. It is a serious matter to willfully practice sin.

RESISTING THE SPIRITS

The sins we tolerate open the door for demonic footholds. But even then, once a believer begins to deal with his sin according to biblical guidelines, Satan's footholds or strongholds crumble. That was Link's experience, and it can be yours—or your child's. I carefully taught Link about the authority he had over Satan through his union with Christ. When voices, taunting, cursing, or other demonic harassments began, Link learned to apply his resistance authority. His torment ceased, and he found freedom. The following prayer is a template for you or your child to use when chronic sin indicates a possible satanic stronghold:

> *In the name of my Lord Jesus Christ and by the power of His blood, I come against the wicked spirit of _____ [name the symptom of spiritual assault] and all its emissaries. I command you to cease your wicked work against me. You and your emissaries must leave me and go where my Lord Jesus Christ sends you. I ask the Holy Spirit to search out all control points of*

my person and evict these dark powers from my presence. I yield my whole person only to the rule and control of my Lord Jesus Christ. I ask the Holy Spirit to sanctify and fully control those areas of my person where the powers of darkness have done their intrusive work.

A resistance of this kind is not a magical incantation or formula. Only the truth applied sets us free from the rule of darkness. Understanding and applying the truth sincerely and consistently leads believers to freedom.

We can compare the actions of wicked spirits to the behavior of spoiled children. Parents have the biblical right to expect and receive obedience from their children. The parent's superior strength certainly helps. But obedience does not happen in all situations, especially when our children are strong willed. Only with persuasive patience and firm discipline will some children respectfully obey.

Wicked spirits are likewise strong willed but even nastier. They receive assignments from their superiors in the kingdom of darkness. They are out to "steal and kill and destroy," according to Jesus (John 10:10). Their task is to rob you of all the Lord has purchased for you in victorious service. Each doggedly seeks to fulfill his assignment, though all know full well that you have authority over them by reason of your union with the person and work of Jesus Christ. But they don't want you to know that. They will not usually obey you when you first use your authority. They will use every available deception and trick to convince you that they are not going to relinquish control.

This is why patient, persistent application of truth is necessary in spiritual warfare. Link followed through by consistently asserting his victory over his flesh and by resisting unclean spirits. A long-term walk of defeat began to turn around. It was not a quick fix, however. Link needed to renounce his generational transfer as well as to consistently apply his freedom in Christ. Once the Adversary places his hooks in us, the return to a walk of freedom is never without opposition.

God's plan for the believer's growth in grace will lead us toward a walk of victory. When Link saw God's plan, he was able to walk faithfully in it.

BEWARE THE KINGDOM OF DARKNESS

Parents who would protect their children need to be free themselves. If a parent fails to establish or reclaim his freedom, an open door of opportunity exists for the Adversary to launch an attack on the parent's offspring. (See Ex. 34:7; Deut. 5:9.)

An important foundation to recapture and maintain personal freedom from the rule of the Evil One is a biblical understanding of our battle. What can help me to stand free from harassment so I can effectively help my child? We must recognize the nature of the opposition we face. A healthy respect and a clear understanding of the kingdom of darkness are essential for us to find spiritual freedom.

Here are three key reminders about Satan's kingdom of darkness. They show us the Adversary has great power. Fortunately, our resources are greater than Satan's. As the apostle John assured us, "The one who is in you [Jesus] is greater than the one who is in the world" (1 John 4:4).

A STRUCTURED KINGDOM SUBJECT TO CHRIST

First, the kingdom of darkness is an organized structure of supernatural evil. It remains part of Christ's creation and is subject to His authority. The Bible tells us, "He is the image of the invisible God, the firstborn over all creation.

For by him all things were created: things in heaven and on earth, visible and invisible, whether thrones or powers or rulers or authorities; all things were created by him and for him. He is before all things, and in him all things hold together" (Col. 1:15–17).

We can in Christ's power stand against the Devil's schemes. Paul wrote, "Put on the full armor of God so that you can take your stand against the devil's schemes. For our struggle is not against flesh and blood, but against the rulers, against the authorities, against the powers of this dark world and against the spiritual forces of evil in the heavenly realms" (Eph. 6:11–12).

Colossians makes clear that Satan is not a creator. Satan himself was created by the hands of the Lord Jesus Christ. The thrones and powers where Satan and his demons roam are still under the full authority of Jesus. Jesus has won the victory over Satan and all the fallen angels. They could not even "consist" (Col. 1:17 NKJV) and hold together apart from the sustaining power of the Creator. For sovereign purposes only God knows, He allows the kingdom of darkness to continue to function until the moment God chooses to judge Satan and his hordes. God will then cast all the fallen spirit beings into the lake of fire He has prepared for them. (See Matt. 25:41; Rev. 20:10.)

AN INFERIOR KINGDOM WITH A COUNTERFEIT PLAN

Second, Satan's kingdom has a counterfeit, parallel plan for nearly everything God does in His perfect plan for redemption. Satan has only temporary influence, but he has a counterfeit plan—a crafty imitation of the real. We must not forget that Satan is exceedingly clever. When he fell in his rebellion, Satan did not lose the gifts and genius that God put into him. He is a master deceiver. Many adjectives describe Satan: Powerful, beautiful, clever, crafty, subtle, deceptive, mighty, ruthless, and sinister are but a few. He is cruel, brutal, angry, manipulative, and mean. He is a destroyer.

The following are five ways his dark kingdom counterfeits everything God has done:

1. **Satan offers a counterfeit family to those who follow him. (See Matt. 13:36–42.)** Jesus illustrated with the parable of the wheat and weeds (Matt. 13:24–30) how clever Satan is to intermingle his family members with the Lord's family (vv. 37–43). Jesus compares them to weeds growing among the wheat. Those who follow Satan will be so plentiful and deceptive that they will even mingle in our churches and will be hard to detect. Like family, they will find much in common as they seek pleasure, independence, and their own approaches to life apart from God.

2. **Satan has created a counterfeit gospel. (See Gal. 1:6–9; 1 Tim. 4:1–3.)** He has his own "good news," which he uses to pervert the ways of truth and enslave the undiscerning. It is a "gospel" of greed, legalism, and perversion. It is even possible to purchase *The Satanic Bible* in some bookstores. New Age teaching, the prosperity gospel, Eastern religions, and quasi-Christian cults like Mormonism, Jehovah's Witnesses, and Christian Science preach a gospel Satan has twisted. The counterfeit gospel of Satan appears in many shapes and sizes. He uses it to pervert and confuse the message of the gospel of Jesus Christ.

3. **Satan has established counterfeit ministers. (See 2 Cor. 10—11.)** A counterfeit gospel must employ messengers. The apostle Paul warns of those who pose as ministers of God and His gospel but are really ministers of the Devil. Their goal is to exalt Satan's realm and destroy the kingdom of God. Paul offers this climactic warning: "his ministers also transform themselves into ministers of righteousness, whose end will be according to their works" (2 Cor. 11:15 NKJV).

4. Satan offers a counterfeit righteousness. (See Rom. 9—10.) Our most serious problems arise when we invent our own righteous standards and ignore the righteousness of God. Such deception has its origin in the master deceiver, Satan himself. Satan continues to mislead people to believe that their own actions done in their own way can please God. In Romans 9 and 10, Paul details the false righteousness that people embrace in lieu of God's true righteousness. A key verse is Romans 10:3 (NKJV): "For they being ignorant of God's righteousness, and seeking to establish their own righteousness, have not submitted to the righteousness of God."

5. Satan seeks his own counterfeit worship. (See 1 Cor. 11:14–33.) Satan's desire to exalt himself as God includes his desire to receive worship, just as God receives worship from those who love Him. The number of people who worship the Devil still surprises me. Yet they are in good company, for Jesus Himself was tempted to worship Satan (Matt. 4:9). The Lord Jesus surely understands that temptation because it came to Him in the wilderness. We must resist such temptation. The answer Jesus gave is still the best: "Away from me, Satan! For it is written: 'Worship the Lord your God, and serve him only'" (Matt. 4:10).

A KINGDOM RULED BY DECEPTION

Third, Satan rules his kingdom by deception, fear, and ignorance. Satan presents no legitimate reality. Everything about him is counterfeit, deceptive, and misleading. Even when he speaks truth, he twists it. He quoted the truth of Scripture in his temptations of the Lord Jesus, but his purpose in doing so was to tempt and deceive. This is still his chief tactic against God's people. Jesus understood that ignorance of the truth can enslave, while knowledge of the truth sets free. So He told His followers, "If you abide in My word, you are

My disciples indeed. And you shall know the truth, and the truth shall make you free.... Therefore if the Son makes you free, you shall be free indeed" (John 8:31–32, 36 NKJV).

Jesus also knew that those who follow Satan are unable to comprehend the things of God. Thus Jesus said to the deluded religious leaders of His day, "Why do you not understand My speech? Because you are not able to listen to My word. You are of your father the devil, and the desires of your father you want to do. He was a murderer from the beginning, and does not stand in the truth, because there is no truth in him. When he speaks a lie, he speaks from his own resources, for he is a liar and the father of it" (John 8:43–44 NKJV).

Deception and fear can succeed only when we are ignorant of the truth. Satan can enslave a believer and his family when they function within the sphere of the Devil's deceptive tactics. Ignorance of truth is as useful to Satan's purposes as the belief of a lie. This is why good Bible teaching and study are so necessary to walk in personal freedom. To protect our children from the rule of darkness, parents must know the truth of their authority so they can apply the truth of God to their children's needs.

Satan is an illusionist. He deceives by offering us a counterfeit life. He uses the world and the media to spread his illusions. Television, videos, movies, the Internet, and the world's music offer a menu of fantasy. They offer a false message about what constitutes the "good life." Revenge becomes a desirable virtue. Sexual conquest is among the greatest achievements. Money and power equal success. The mysteries of occult power are exciting and worthy of pursuit. Such are the illusions of Satan.

Satan's kingdom is behind the perversion of Judeo-Christian values. Godly Christian parents are all that stand between their children and Satan's plans for their children.

PARENTS' SPIRITUAL AUTHORITY

Lance and Betty Faith are spiritually mature believers. They served several years as missionaries. Lance is now an elder in his church. It was my privilege to have a part in training them for victory over the world, the flesh, and the Devil. They have become faithful warriors.

Despite their faithful service, however, their son, Max, became a spiritual rebel. Lance and Betty blamed many of their son's problems on their lives before they became Christians. Having come to faith in Christ later in life, they were aware that Max had suffered from the fallout of their own sinful rebellions. They feared that as a young boy he absorbed some of their stubborn example.

Lance and Betty kept praying and soliciting the prayers of their Christian friends on behalf of Max. There was little progress. Max asserted his independence, acting out in sinful ways. The result was a disastrous personal life and a fractured relationship with his parents that lasted for seven long years.

"It was a lonely, painful time," confessed Lance. "It was like a desert. Our expectations were low and hope was almost lost."

God was at work, however. Lance began to review his own responsibility before God. He gained insights about his generational tie to his son. An intense review of Satan's limits and the Scripture's truths accomplished a breakthrough. First, a study of Hebrews 7:1–10 opened Lance's eyes to a new concept. One text, in particular, stood out.

> Now the law requires the descendants of Levi who become priests to collect a tenth from the people— that is, their brothers—even though their brothers are descended from Abraham.... In the one case, the tenth is collected by men who die; but in the other

case, by him who is declared to be living. One might even say that Levi, who collects the tenth, paid the tenth through Abraham, because when Melchizedek met Abraham, Levi was still in the body of his ancestor. (vv. 5, 8–10)

Though this text emphasizes the superiority of the Melchizedek priesthood over the Aaronic priesthood, Lance recognized something else. The whole line of reasoning had its basis in two phrases: "descended from Abraham" and "still in the body of his ancestor." Lance saw in a new way how close his own tie was to Max. Lance wrote the following account of what he learned.

I reviewed spiritual warfare concerning Satan's holds or rights to my son. It slowly came to me that I, too, had rights in my son's life. I [began] to investigate them. I discovered that as his father, I had the following rights:

1. Through Moses, my Lord Jesus Christ commanded me to train my son to walk according to Scripture (Deut. 4:9).

2. Through the apostle Paul, Jesus instructed me to train and admonish my son according to the Scriptures (Eph. 6:4).

3. Through Solomon, the Lord Jesus Christ admonished me to rear my son in dedication to the Lord. I must teach him how to live his life so that it would please the Lord. I was responsible to motivate my son to want to carry out all of the Lord's Word in his spiritual life (Prov. 22:6; 29:17).

4. Through Paul and by Jesus' own example, He instructed me to love Max unconditionally and continually (1 Cor. 13:4–13).

Seeing these precepts triggered deeper spiritual awareness. I saw that Satan had gained the ground or right to rule in my son's soul and over his emotions, intellect, and will. His sinful lifestyle and rebellion granted those rights. But I also saw that I as his father had a bond and spiritual priesthood in Max's life that had been established by Jesus Christ. I knew that it was up to Betty and me to carry out these God-given rights to help our son find freedom. As ambassadors of Jesus Christ, we could enter the battle on our son's behalf to help regain the lost territory.

Lance engaged the Lord in intensive prayer. There he spoke out against the realm of wicked spirits that had direct or indirect rights to rule over his son. "As a Christian believer and as Max's father, I commanded them to hear me without responding by any overt activity. I reviewed against them my rights as expressed in the above four points. I affirmed strongly that Max, as the fruit of his mother's womb and my loins, was given only to Jesus Christ, our Lord and Savior. I then confessed all known sin of my son to my heavenly Father as Job and Nehemiah had done (Job 1:5; Neh. 1:6), asking the Lord to claim back all the ground given through the merit of His blood."

Lance's prayer was powerful and confident:

In the name of my Lord Jesus Christ, I bind the evil powers assigned to rule Max from the full use of their power over Max. By faith, I affirm that I have planted Jehovah Nissi's* banner in the center of my son's soul. I command that all demons assigned to rule

*and destroy Max must daily see that banner of
Jehovah's ownership over his life.*

Then Max's father prayed that God would cover his son
with the person of the Holy Spirit "like a blanket assigned to
bring him back to the reality of God's truth."
Lance "was particularly concerned that Max would know
what God expected of him and would be aware that God's
wrath is very real." His description continues.

> Daily we entered into this kind of prayer battle. Betty
> and I prayed along the list outlined above, expecting
> the Holy Spirit to apply His perfect doctrinal under-
> standing as He brought our prayers to the Father. We
> affirmed that we were praying in the will of our
> Savior in accord with our responsibility to our son
> (1 John 5:14–15).
>
> Compared to the seven years we had waited, within
> a short passage of time, our son's life began to
> change. At first it was a glimmer of hope, but it grew
> to a complete reversal of his rebellious, indifferent
> spiritual attitudes and ways. The light of the Lord
> slowly rekindled. His eyes returned from a glare of
> defiance and challenge to a sparkle of love.
>
> Our son is now walking with Jesus as his Lord. He
> exhibits significant signs of Christlike growth. As my
> wife and I took our stand on God's Word and poured
> out continuous, unconditional love on our son, God
> honored our total, unexplainable faith. We were con-
> vinced that Christ's defeat of the powers of darkness
> in our son's life was total. We saw and are still seeing
> it happen. Jesus Christ was and is victorious!

EXERCISE YOUR
GOD-GIVEN POSITION OF
PROTECTIVE AUTHORITY
IN THE CHILD'S LIFE,
AND EVEN THE MOST
RESISTANT STRONGHOLDS
OF EVIL WILL BE FORCED
TO RETREAT.

9

Spiritistic Activity in Children

T odd seemed to be a resourceful child and quite capable
of creative invention in his patterns of play. In fact, he
became so creative that he enjoyed playing by himself more
than playing with his siblings or friends. When he played by
himself, his mother often heard him carrying on a conversation with an imaginary friend who played with him. His
mother attributed his talking to his creative imagination and
gift for fantasy. She saw no hint of danger until one day she
overheard him talking in a conversational tone that seemed
to indicate that Todd was actually hearing verbal responses in
his conversation with his imaginary playmate.

Todd's mother later confessed her concern but did not
think it important enough to warrant further investigation.
Other events in Todd's life gradually emerged, however, that
indicated a troubled son who needed help.

Horrible nightmares would awaken Todd during his
sleep. They were often so frightening and realistic that he
would tremble from head to toe. While he recovered from
the dream, he typically would remain in a trancelike state,

neither awake nor asleep. Attempts to awaken him were fruitless, and though the eight-year-old would cling to his parents, they couldn't communicate with him. He seemed to be staring into the distance at some fearful scene.

Todd would also talk in his sleep in what sounded like actual conversation, though his parents could hear only Todd's side of the exchange. He would then awaken in a fearful state. Prayer was vital to the recovery process. When Todd woke up during these fearful experiences, his parents would immediately begin to pray authoritatively. As his parents prayed, Todd would frequently cease his trembling and fall back to sleep.

Todd's story demonstrates some of the results of spiritistic activities parents may observe in their children's lives. I met Todd's parents at one of the spiritual warfare conferences I led. Their journey into spiritual warfare began with Todd's experiences. They both felt an "evil presence" whenever their child awoke in sheer terror and wondered if his issues could be demonic. They looked for good reading material on the subject in their local Christian bookstore and read *The Adversary*, my first book on spiritual warfare. They consistently and aggressively utilized the principles of authority I teach in that book, and as a result, have seen Todd gain freedom from both his dreams and his imaginary friend.

This family's experience introduces us to the practical benefits of biblically balanced spiritual warfare. Without psychological counseling or professional help of any kind, these parents used spiritual principles to help their hurting son. Some children do not respond as quickly and effectively to biblical warfare as Todd did, but there is a common thread that runs through all such experiences. Spiritual resources demand a place of priority in every believer's life. We have often looked too quickly to the secular world for answers and have neglected the proper use of the weapons of spiritual warfare. Even when medical or psychological help may be necessary to fully resolve a difficult problem, we must be sure to give attention to the proper use of our spiritual resources.

TODD'S IMAGINARY FRIEND

As they conversed with their son, Todd's parents concluded his imaginary friend was actually a spirit entity. Todd says he actually saw a "boylike figure." He was usually nice to Todd, but at other times would threaten and coerce him to do things that Todd didn't like. He also would appear at night in some of Todd's dreams and say disturbing things that introduced fear and confusion into Todd's life.

Todd was reluctant at first to give up his friend, but prayer changed that. As his parents began to lead him in protective prayers at bedtime to claim God's shielding from intrusive demonic activity, two things happened. The horrible nightmares and terror experiences stopped. But Todd's "play friend" also became more abusive in his conversations with Todd. He expressed anger at Todd for revealing their "secret."

The parents instructed their son to command his "friend" to leave in the name of the Lord Jesus Christ. Todd learned to resist this "friend" and to use authority over him. To Todd's delight the abusive words stopped, and the "friend" stopped his visits. His fear vanished with his use of spiritual resources, and this young boy learned to resist his enemy.

Parents, however, must exercise discernment. Please do not conclude that your child's friend is a demon. A child's imaginary friend may be just that—an imaginary friend. My children and grandchildren have played with imaginary friends. Such play can be a normal and healthy part of a child's development. Fantasy may display a child's capacity for creativity through active imagination. We must always keep a proper balance in our perspective, or we may do unnecessary harm to the ones we long to protect.

When should we suspect demonic influence? Communication is an important ingredient in any evaluation. In Todd's case, communication began to reveal something evil occurring in their son's life. When they learned that their son's "friend" actually appeared at times and sometimes talked to Todd in threatening language, they knew something was not right. The accompanying nightmares and trancelike states and the sensation of an evil presence provided additional evidence.

A WORD OF CAUTION

One hesitates in a chapter like this to suggest areas that may evidence spiritistic activity in the lives of our children. If you are skeptical that spiritistic activities will occur in your own child, good. If we misinterpret or misuse such "evidences," they may lead us to see demons as the effective cause behind every difficulty. We become "spiritual neurotics" who convey to our children a superstitious preoccupation with demons and wicked spirits. Young children will respond in fear to such an unbalanced approach to life. Worse yet, as our children grow older they may dismiss the issue of spiritual warfare with a laugh of scorn, the paranoid preoccupation of "religious fanatics." Part of Satan's strategy is to discredit any instruction that teaches others how to resist him. Be wise, prudent, and prayerful whenever you approach spiritual warfare on behalf of your children.

I recall occasions when a concerned parent brought a troubled child to me, asking me to cast a demon out of him. That usually indicated that the parent had already conveyed to the child that he was demon possessed. There are few things that a parent can do to harm a child more and make him more vulnerable to the deceiver's work. Such unwise communication conveys false guilt, rejection, and diminishes a child's self-worth.

The child thinks, *My parents believe I'm really bad and the Devil has me. I'm no good and I'll never be worth anything.* The Devil's helpers will reinforce that faulty perception with all of the deceptive tools available to them.

Children are highly impressionable, and parents must maintain a constant, protective sensitivity as they help them through their struggles. Even when there is strong evidence of demonic control in a child's life, it's best not to work directly with the child in any kind of confrontation procedure. The best place to begin is to prayerfully guard your child's freedom. Exercise your God-given position of protective authority in the child's life, and even the most resistant strongholds of evil will be forced to retreat. Grandparents and even close Christian friends can also exercise their protective authority over a troubled child in prayer. Remember, you have authority.

Maintaining Your Balance

Todd's parents provide a model of parental intervention. Without alarming Todd and with careful study, they learned how to exercise biblically balanced spiritual warfare. Prayer intervention stopped the nighttime trances. Protective prayer before bedtime ended the troubling nightmares. Conversations during sleep also ceased. Through prayer and patient communication, the Lord helped them to teach their son to resist spiritistic activity without frightening or harming him. They modeled spiritual wisdom that deserves our attention.

Cathy was not so fortunate. She experienced nightmares and displayed behavior patterns that caused her parents to suspect spiritual oppression. They took Cathy when she was seven to a healing meeting, hoping to gain help for her. The healer professed to have the gift of "discernment," the ability to heal and cast out demons. In a highly emotional state, the healer laid hands on Cathy, named the demon, and commanded him to leave her. Cathy fell to the floor in a trancelike state, and the healer pronounced her "delivered" from the demon.

Cathy, now an adult, explained how the whole experience had left her with fears and torments she was afraid to share with her parents. She was afraid they might take her to such a meeting again. The experience had contributed to a downward path in her life. Cathy turned inward to heal her hurts. She tried to forget and find help in pleasure. She withdrew from her parents and her faith. Rebellion, sinful living, and occult experimentation reduced her life to a shambles of confusion and deeper bondage to powers of darkness. She came to me in a desperate search for help to gain her freedom from the powers of darkness that still tormented her.

What does Cathy's experience tell us? It emphasizes the fact that, though miraculous healing is still part of God's program today, we must be careful how we seek that healing. The Word of God warns us that the chief manifestations of deception at "the end of the age" will be "counterfeit miracles, signs and wonders" (2 Thess. 2:9–12). Other passages, such as Matthew 7:21–23; 24:24–25; and Revelation 13:13–14, further underscore the danger of such deceptions. These works will be so impressive that even some of the practitioners themselves will not realize they are tapping in to occult powers (Matt. 7:21–23). The deceptions will be so clever that they will have power to deceive even believers. (See Matt. 24:24.)

We are living in a day with an intense interest in the supernatural. We need, therefore, to exercise great wisdom and caution. Eastern religions, New Age mysticism, and overt satanism all have power to effect supernatural healings. God certainly has the sovereign right to perform miracles. And when He does perform them, we rejoice. We must, however, remain alert to the counterfeits. They are one of the chief tools that Satan uses in his final effort to deceive the masses and rule the world. The authenticity of the gospel has already been firmly established. The death, burial, and resurrection of our Lord Jesus Christ authenticate the message we proclaim. History affirms that truth. By divine revelation, we have it fully recorded in all its detail in our Bibles. We need no more than that. Everyone who has been saved thus far came to Christ because of that gospel message, and everyone who will be saved will come for the same reason. (See Rom. 1:16; 1 Cor. 15:1–11.)

ANGELS ON OUR SIDE

God also created spirit beings called angels. They were all holy and righteous in the original creation. He created each angel for a specific purpose and assigned them various levels of rank, authority, and power. (See Eph. 6:12; Col. 1:16–17.) Lucifer (Satan's original name) may have been the most powerful of all the angelic host. He was certainly one of the highest ranking angels. The Bible seems to indicate that only the archangel Michael, and perhaps Gabriel, possessed a rank equal to that of Lucifer.

When Lucifer rebelled against God, he drew one-third of the created angels into his rebellious scheme to take over God's position (Rev. 12:4; see also the outline in chapter 6, "Redeemed Persons Facing Satan's Kingdom"). These "fallen angels" continue to function in their created rank and authority, but instead of doing the will of God, they serve the

Devil, whose name God changed from Lucifer ("angel of light") to Satan ("adversary").

The original task of all the angels was to serve God and God's people "who will inherit salvation" (Heb. 1:14). Since Satan's rebellion, he and his fallen angels (demons) work to oppose God's kingdom and to undermine the credibility and ministry of those who follow Jesus Christ.

But let us remember that God has a dual purpose for His holy angels. Good angels guard believers from the schemes of the Devil, who seeks to harm them. They also assist God's people to maintain a victorious Christian walk. Jesus told His earliest followers, "I have given you authority to trample on snakes and scorpions and to overcome all the power of the enemy" (Luke 10:19). It is in God's plans to crush Satan under the feet of believers (Rom. 16:20).

Satan uses his fallen angels to rob us of freedom and to destroy us (John 10:10), but the holy angels continue to minister to and protect God's children. Those good angels are valuable allies in our struggle against the Adversary.

A spiritual battle presently rages between the fallen and the holy angels. It's all-out war. Just as the major work of holy angels is to minister to and care for the redeemed, the principal activity of fallen angels is to attack, defeat, and destroy the redeemed.[1] The challenge to live a godly life involves a spiritual struggle that the apostle Paul called a wrestling match (Eph. 6:12).

My purpose in reminding us of the ministry of angels at this point is to illustrate again why parents need to be on their guard. There is a diabolical conspiracy between spirit beings to rob, kill, and destroy us and our children. Our protective resources are awesome in God's grace, but we must not take for granted that protection. We are wisely and aggressively to use those resources to assist and protect our children.

EVIDENCE OF SPIRITISTIC ACTIVITY IN OUR CHILDREN

How can we recognize spiritistic activity in our children's lives? The following section highlights some common signs. Bear in mind that the list is not exhaustive, nor does it provide a definitive "diagnosis." If one or more of these signs appear in your child, do not automatically conclude that demons have gained access to your son or daughter. But the appearance of several of these symptoms *may* mean your child is under attack. It should alert us to pray authoritatively and to "wrestle" on their behalf.

ABNORMAL FEARS AND PHOBIAS

Fear is probably the Devil's favorite weapon. In fact, the fear of Satan is the exact opposite of faith in God. Faith pleases and activates the Lord's response toward believers. Without faith it is impossible to please God, but faith pleases Him greatly. (See Heb. 11.) Fear activates and pleases the Devil because it is the opposite of faith. The lion roars to immobilize his victims, and Satan roars to paralyze us (1 Peter 5:8). When a child's life is characterized by fear, we may suspect the Devil is at work. When Satan's work meets defeat, the fear tends to vanish.

Abnormal fears in our children should prompt a parent to begin to pray against any demonic powers that seek to rule that child.

PATTERNS OF OUT-OF-CONTROL ANGER AND FITS OF RAGE

In its various forms and expressions, anger appears in each list that catalogs the sins of the flesh in the New Testament. (See Matt. 15:9–20; Mark 7:20–23; Gal. 5:19–21; Col. 3:5–14.) Ephesians 4:26–27 also warns that the willful practice of anger gives "place to the devil." Out-of-control anger may be a symptom of a spiritistic influence or even ruling control.

Ned was an angry little boy. Big for his age, he manipulated and controlled his mother with his violent fits of rage. He would flail at her with his fists and kick her with his heavy shoes. Discipline was ineffective; it only made his rages worse. It wasn't until his mother recognized that she was dealing with more than an angry son that Ned began to change. Her consistent prayer against the attempt of a spirit of anger to rule over her son began to free him from his violent, angry behavior.

APPARITIONS AND VOICES

Tom, the young son of a pastor, would often enter his parents' room in sheer terror and complain of seeing a sinister face in the dark. Thinking their son was just having a nightmare, the parents would allow him into bed with them until he fell back to sleep. The father would then carry Tom back to his own bed, and usually he would sleep through the rest of the night. The frequency of these experiences increased until one night the little fellow complained there were "two of them." Still convinced that it was just a nightmare, the father walked his son back to the room. As they neared the door, the father heard voices in the room and felt cold chills sweep over him. As he pushed the door open, he saw two dark, shadowy figures quickly disappear.

The father knelt by his son's bed and asked the Lord to protect his son from any such appearances. A consistent practice of prayer saw the elimination of such unwelcome visits from the realm of darkness. (This experience reminds us not to dismiss too quickly a child's account of an "appearance" of some sort or of voices speaking when no one is around.)

For a younger child, it is best that parents not make a fuss in the child's presence. But the parent should take a protective approach in prayer and forbid all powers of darkness from making any visits. It's appropriate also to ask the Lord to assign His holy angels to guard against such intrusions into our homes and lives. Protective prayer is effective and disrupts the plans of darkness. (See the sample prayer for a child hearing voices or seeing images in appendix 2.)

When a child has received the Lord Jesus Christ and is more mature, intrusive spiritistic activity can provide an opportunity to train that child in resisting the Devil and his schemes. Spirit powers seek to rule through fear and foreboding. The appearance of an apparition would frighten most adult Christians, let alone children. But a deliberate, prayerful approach will help a child to know he possesses the authority to resist and will equip him with the proper words to pray.

Don't allow supernatural experiences to intimidate either you or your children. If you know what to do, you will not need to fear the unknown, and you will be able to use such unpleasant experiences as tools for the spiritual development of your children.

CRUEL TREATMENT OF ANIMALS OR PLAYMATES

King David prayed, "Consider my enemies, for they are many; and they hate me with cruel hatred" (Ps. 25:19 NKJV). As David mentions these many enemies, he refers to their use of brutal cruelty; he might be referring to the realm of supernatural evil. Cruelty is a part of most forms of evil, but it has particular significance when you face the Devil.

Those who counsel the demonically oppressed should remember what a ruthlessly cruel enemy the Devil is. Cruelty is the antithesis of the fruit of the Holy Spirit and one of the strongest evidences of Satan's rule. My experience as a pastor and counselor has been that most people who come out of satanism do so because they suffer and hurt so much. The Devil rules by means of cruelty. As people descend into evil, the powers of darkness increase their control by affliction with suffering. The victim experiences relief only when he or she conforms.

Perhaps that's enough to suggest why cruelty to animals or toward siblings and playmates should arouse our concern. The powers of darkness sometimes use cruelty to manipulate a child.

INTENSE HATRED

Hate is the opposite of love. The apostle John wrote, "Whoever does not love does not know God, because God is love" (1 John 4:8). If God is love, then Satan is hate. Hatred characterizes his rule.

Little Jennifer didn't appreciate correction. Even mild discipline led to expressions of intense hatred, usually focused on her mother. A dark countenance would come over her as she clenched her teeth and screamed, "I hate you! I hate you! I hate you!"

When Jennifer was in her time-out chair, her mother would hear her muttering, "I hate myself! I hate my looks! I hate my room!" Feelings of hate were always close to the surface. If anything displeased Jennifer, the hate scenario would start again. Her mother confided, "When I see that hatred in her eyes, it frightens me."

Jennifer's parents knew there was something abnormal about their daughter's preoccupation with hatred, but they did not link her behavior to spiritistic influences until they read Neil T. Anderson's book *The Seduction of Our Children* (Harvest House, 1991). The parents began to intercede for their daughter with protective prayer and in time saw her change in response to their application of warfare principles. They had no doubt Jennifer had been under demonic assault.

Like cruelty, intense hatred arises from satanic influence and involvement. Jennifer's parents were wise to recognize the source of their daughter's hatred.

Other Evidences of Spiritistic Activity

We've examined the five major evidences of spiritistic activity in children. But there are others we would be wise to be aware of. Parents must learn to recognize these symptoms and to practice the same warfare principles that Jennifer's parents learned. Additional symptoms to watch for include the following:

- Trancelike states of sleep, sleepwalking, sleep talking, or holding conversations while in a trancelike state that the child does not later remember
- Compulsive behavior patterns of lying, stealing, cursing, hitting, fighting, laughing, crying, pinching, pounding of the head on a wall
- Physical maladies that seems to unexplainably "morph" into some other disorder or painful sensations that migrate to other areas of the body—be sure to seek medical attention for these conditions and consider the possibility of an illness. But be wise; the Adversary could be at work.
- A preoccupation with blood, death, feces, fire, or violence. Billy seemed from infancy to have an attraction to feces. He smeared it on everything whenever he had the chance. Interests in blood and fire eventually replaced his preoccupation with fecal material, and television violence fascinated him. These were clues that pointed to spiritual oppression. His parents began to apply spiritual warfare principles, and Billy gained relief from these destructive patterns.
- Clairvoyance, premonitions, extrasensory perception (ESP), or other supernatural "gifts" that emerge. Such gifts usually are generational and signal occult activity that some family member in the generational lineage has practiced.

◻ Cutting and self-mutilation. Those troubled by the powers of darkness often resort to actions that bring harm to themselves. Cutting of oneself is as old as the biblical accounts. (See Mark 5; 1 Kings 18:28.) A proneness to self-injury may signal spiritistic control.

◻ Withdrawal from family and friends. A desire for silence and solitude can be healthy, but it is cause for concern when coupled with abrupt mood swings, rejection of loved ones, loneliness, suspicion, and fear. Fantasies about imaginary friends, places, and events may accompany a move into isolation and withdrawal that is connected to demonic activity.

◻ Inability to concentrate and learn even when average and above-average abilities are evident. The inability of the human mind to receive or express information may be symptomatic of a learning disability that requires the attention of a professional. But it can also indicate the works of darkness. God is not the author of confusion, but the Devil delights to produce confusion; he will impair understanding in every way he can. When a child is diagnosed with attention-deficit/hyperactivity disorder (ADHD) or some other learning disorder, in addition to medical treatment, protective warfare prayer should be part of the healing strategy.

◻ Interest in ghosts, magic, occultism, fortune-telling, and similar fare. Occult activity in its many forms is a tool the Enemy regularly uses. A child's interest in such things may signal the manipulative attempt of wicked spirits to gain ground against a child.

◻ Aberrant sexual interests or activity. Early masturbation, fascination with pornography, and use of obscene language may signal the invisible works of evil powers.

◻ Inability to give or accept gestures of kindness and love. When a child rejects love, it generally signals an emotional problem, but it may also signal demonic influence. God is love, and as previously mentioned, Satan does not love. He hates. The practice of warfare prayer and principles should become a top priority when a child can neither accept nor give love.

◻ Destructive acts. Satan and his workers are destroyers. Children suffering manipulation by powers of darkness may manifest destructive behavior. If a child deliberately breaks things, the behavior may indicate influence from evil, destructive powers. In some cases, children will even smash toys that they formerly treated as personal treasures.

◻ Extreme depression and expressed thoughts of suicide. Suicide remains one of the major causes of death among young people. There is justifiable concern about the increase in this disturbing phenomenon. Jesus once ascribed to Satan the role of murderer. He said to His critics who were out to kill Him, "You belong to your father, the devil, and you want to carry out your father's desire. He was a murderer from the beginning, not holding to the truth, for there is no truth in him. When he lies, he speaks his native language, for he is a liar and the father of lies" (John 8:44). When anyone takes his own life, the deceiver and the murderer is somehow at work. According to Hebrews 2:14, he has "the power of death." The normal human desire built into us by our Creator is to fight for survival.

◻ Sleep problems. When I've counseled an obviously demonized person, he will frequently yawn and tend to drift off to sleep. The same thing will happen when

I read to him the Bible or when we are praying. Offer a resisting prayer, and such behavior will likely stop. Other sleep problems include graphic nightmares, restless tossing during sleep, and insomnia.

◻ Extreme rebellion in the face of discipline. God commands loving parents to discipline their children. God, Himself, disciplines us as His children. (See Prov. 13:24; Heb. 12:1–15.) The rejection of discipline may well suggest the activity of evil influence. A violent and rebellious response to discipline may be due to spiritistic influence.

◻ Inability to enjoy play and laughter. Fun, play, games, and laughter come as naturally to children as breathing. No sooner did the bombing and artillery shelling cease in Sarajevo than the children were out in the streets to laugh and play, even in the rubble. When a child cannot enjoy play, something dark may be taking place. Satan seeks to rob children of laughter.

◻ The appearance of occult and satanic symbols on a child's books, clothing, possessions, or body. Satan's goal is to make children willing participants in his programs of evil. He seeks to draw them into experimentation with the supernatural. A parent may want to seek other resources that deal with the occult.[2] Every parent should develop sufficient awareness of Satan's entrapments to know the evidences of even superficial interests on the part of his or her child. For instance, a subtle interest in certain types of music that glorify the occult may be part of an early stage. Books or articles about séances, curses, rituals, and magical potions are a part of the reading materials of one feeling an attraction to supernatural evil.

THE PROPER RESPONSE TO
SPIRITISTIC ACTIVITY IN CHILDREN

If you observe in your children one or more of the previous signs of possible spiritistic influence, what should you do? Here are some suggestions:

BE CALM

Fear and panic are tools Satan uses to rule and destroy. The Lord Jesus Christ has given all born-again believers all the power and authority we need to overcome darkness and protect our children.

KEEP A BIBLICAL BALANCE

Remember Cathy's parents? Don't seek out a "faith healer" or "expert in spiritual warfare" to cast out demons from your child. Such a sensational approach can be harmful to a child. Don't opt for a quick fix. Pursue a biblical approach and apply spiritual truth and parental protection to your child.

TALK TO YOUR PASTOR OR ANOTHER CHRISTIAN LEADER YOU RESPECT

Express your concerns. Describe the battle and enlist his prayer support.

PRACTICE DAILY PREVAILING PRAYER

The sample prayers in the appendixes will offer guidance and insight on using your authority to resist the Enemy.

LIST THE SYMPTOMS THAT CONCERN YOU

It will increase the effectiveness of your prayerful intercession. It can also assist you as you directly address the powers of darkness and exercise your parental authority.

Before you apply this final suggestion to confront the power of darkness through prayer, prepare yourself spiritually.

Take a day to fast and pray for the Lord to grant you wisdom and courage as you use your authority in Christ to free your child from the harassment of dark powers. You may also want to work through the steps to freedom that you will find in the next chapter.

SELECT A TIME WHEN YOU WILL BE ABLE TO MAINTAIN A QUIET AND UNINTERRUPTED PRAYER FOCUS FOR AT LEAST THIRTY MINUTES

If your bedroom is in the general proximity of a sleeping child, that may be the best place and time for such a direct confrontation. It will be helpful, whenever possible, for both parents to pray together, but a single parent need not be fearful. It is our Lord's authority that provides protection and freedom.

In appendix 3 you will find a sample prayer that addresses possible demonic influence on your child. I recommend you either use it or develop a similar specific prayer for protection against any powers of darkness you suspect are harassing your child. The prayer calls on Jesus to bind demonic forces and to remove any lingering forces of evil that could deceive your child. The prayer also calls on the Holy Spirit to sanctify the child's whole person for service.

The wholehearted recitation of truth, as well as a declaration of the believer's authority to resist evil activity, serves to honor God and to weaken evil. When you use the steps to freedom and other procedures presented in this book, the freeing process will be both effective and powerful. Parents may want to repeat this procedure on successive occasions. We must be sure to close every door of opportunity for enemy activity. The Lord commands us to be vigilant in our warfare (Eph. 6:18).

10

Applying the Seven Steps to Freedom

T he transfer of blessings—and disasters—from one generation to the next makes for a fascinating study in the Old Testament. The biblical accounts make the linkage between the previous generations' action and the descendants' behavior quite clear. This is especially obvious in the biblical records of the kings of Israel and Judah who reigned from after Solomon to the captivity of Israel and Judah. Bad kings spawned more bad kings; breaking the pattern was not easy. Among the rulers of Judah, only five kings fully honored God after Solomon; most were influenced to evil by their wayward parents.

When the king served God in a pleasing manner, the Bible cites a clear link to David—a man after God's own heart—or to some other God-fearing man in the king's generational lineage. For instance, twice in 2 Chronicles the Bible compares a good king to King David: "He did what was right in the eyes of the LORD, just as his father David had done" (29:2; cf. 34:2). When a king follows sinful ways, we invariably see a link to someone wicked in the king's generational lineage. For instance, "Amon was twenty-two years old when he became king, and he reigned in Jerusalem two years. He did evil in the eyes of the LORD, as his father Manasseh had done" (2 Chron. 33:21–22).

Wickedness and disobedience seem to transfer from father to son, or to some other person within the family tree. Faith, obedience, and godly conduct almost always have a generational tie to godly individuals who have gone before them.

Perhaps as a parent you worry that the sins and rebelliousness of your own parents or previous generations have affected your life, as well as your ability to raise your children to be godly. You wonder, *How do I begin to undo all of the rubble from my personal and family failures?* Your concern is a good sign, showing your desire to change. Change is possible for you as a child of God. But how?

CHANGE IS POSSIBLE

As we noted earlier, the transfer of ancestral wickedness or generational godliness is not automatic or irreversible. The patterns of earlier generations are not, after all, like original sin. This truth aligns with the recognition of individual responsibility as well as the opportunities a loving God repeatedly provides for our repentance and His grace.

Let's return to the long line of kings in the Old Testament to demonstrate this. Manasseh, one of the later kings of Judah, was perhaps the most wicked. Through His prophets the Lord said, "Manasseh ... has done more evil than the Amorites who preceded him" (2 Kings 21:11). The catalog of his sins includes such abominable practices as sacrificing his sons to heathen gods in the Valley of Ben Hinnom, a dreadful form of Molech worship in which parents would hand over their firstborn to be roasted as a sacrifice inside a red-hot idol. He also promoted the worst forms of witchcraft, sorcery, fortune-telling, and magical occult practices. As an additional insult toward God, he even introduced his wickedness to the sacred temple set apart for worship of the God of Israel. In his folly, we read that he "led Judah and the people of Jerusalem astray, so that they did more evil than the nations the LORD had destroyed before the Israelites" (2 Chron. 33:9). Despite such evil, the Lord showed great patience toward Manasseh. Although the text doesn't say why, it may be that God's patience was due to the godly life of his father, the good King Hezekiah. We see a shining example of God's mercy in the way the Lord dealt with Manasseh when the Assyrian army invaded Judah. The Assyrians captured Manasseh and led him away in disgrace with his hands tightly bound in shackles and a chain attached to a hook through his nose. Even so, we must take note of a brief description of God's gracious goodness to Manasseh.

> In his distress he sought the favor of the LORD his God and humbled himself greatly before the God of his fathers. And when he prayed to him, the LORD was moved by his entreaty and listened to his plea; so he brought him back to Jerusalem and to his kingdom. Then Manasseh knew that the LORD is God. (2 Chron. 33:12–13)

That is an example of God's amazing grace and astounding mercy. And because of God's goodness, Manasseh followed through with his commitment. He launched a thorough cleanup of the moral pollution that abounded in Jerusalem, the temple, and throughout the nation of Judah. Repentance saved his reign from total disaster. He finished his long rule with comparative prosperity and peace. When he died, the nation gave him an honorable burial and put his son Amon on the throne.

Amon's reign lasted only two years. The sinful patterns his father had modeled throughout his life continued to find their expression in Amon. He never repented of them. His own household servants finally assassinated him, and his eight-year-old son, Josiah, ascended to the throne. Josiah, in radical contrast, was a godly king who instituted one of the greatest reforms the nation had experienced since the days of Samuel and David.

The history of Hezekiah and his descendants further emphasizes the point: No matter how wicked a family line has been, we can experience repentance, forgiveness, and a reversal of generational sin. Genuine repentance is the key. Even as Manasseh found forgiveness and miraculous restoration through God's grace, the scars of his sins corrupted his son's reign. But Manasseh's eventual faith and prayers, and those of his father, Hezekiah, brought generational blessings. Their respective grandson and great-grandson, Josiah, was one of Judah's most godly reformers.

The healing power that results from saving faith, godly repentance, and faithful prayer finds no scar or obstacle too large to remove. Neither generational sin nor any other kind of wickedness can cancel the power of the gospel to transform generational curses into blessings.

Regardless of your personal or generational background, healing, forgiveness, and freedom are available in God's grace and mercy. The finished work of Christ can conquer the farthest reaches of wickedness and evil and can forever remove their generational consequences.

Let's explore further how to apply freedom to yourself so you can raise your children in a home of spiritual strength.

THE PLACE TO BEGIN

You may have started strong in your commitment to Christ, but now your joy has faded. Your peace has gone. You wonder what you're missing. Why all the stress? Defeats and the trash of failure clutter your life. You feel as if you've lost your way. You're fairly confident about your salvation, but your walk with God is a mess. Your problem may be linked to the influences of past generations. Even if it is not, you will want to change your sinful patterns so you may raise your children in a godly home.

In chapter 12 of *The Bondage Breaker* (Harvest House, 1990), Neil T. Anderson's fine book on spiritual warfare, the author presents several steps to freedom. I recommend the book, which will serve as a helpful resource. We recognize the greatest value of these steps to freedom when God brings spiritual renewal to His church. Perverted sexuality, widespread occultism, abusive parenting, drug usage, homes broken by divorce, and so many other sins have opened people's lives to demonic afflictions. When those with such backgrounds come to know Jesus Christ as Savior and Lord, disciples would serve new believers well by helping each one to walk through the steps to freedom.

The following is my personal adaptation of Anderson's freedom steps. A word of qualification is in order here. Demonic torment in a believer's life is not the norm. It can happen only when a person has yielded significant ground to the kingdom of darkness. When we yield ground to the Enemy, we must take it back, and it begins with renunciation. It can be a painstaking process to discover what areas of ground we have ceded to the Enemy, but the following steps to freedom will help facilitate that process.

PREPARING FOR THE SEVEN STEPS TO FREEDOM

The following steps cover the major ways believers give ground to darkness. Parents will do well to go through the steps to freedom for their own spiritual benefit. There may also be times when you will need to lead your child through these important steps. But take great care. We cannot force such action on our child. It is sometimes wise for a trusted leader or godly friend, instead of a parent, to be the one to help that young person.

One can go through the steps alone, but I've found that the presence of a spiritually alert counselor or friend is of great benefit. Their prayer support, protective assistance, and confidentiality provide a helpful spiritual atmosphere.

Proper Preparation. A quiet place relatively free from the possibility of interruption is important. A time frame of two to three hours may be necessary. Avoid a hurried atmosphere. Preparation should include opportunity to work through each area, making a list of all matters that require examination. Some may wish to precede the session with a period of prayer and fasting.

Believers need to grasp the importance of this procedure. Finding freedom from demonic influence is important for two reasons. First, it gives us personal freedom. Many believers have given ground to the kingdom of darkness by past sinful practices. It is a spiritually healthy exercise to systematically confess and renounce areas that have granted a demonic claim against us. Repentance is a noble practice. It honors God and frees people. Second, the procedure provides a transferable tool. Every believer should learn to help another believer to claim the freedom Christ has won for him.

An Essential Foundation. Before we begin, we must be sure the proper foundation exists. Each participant in a freedom session must be sure of his or her own personal salvation through faith in Christ. Are you trusting Jesus Christ alone for the forgiveness of your sins and the assurance of eternal life? I often urge participants besieged by doubts to answer Satan's accusations with a positive affirmation:

*I affirm that my only hope for the forgiveness of
my sins and eternal life rests on the finished work of*

*my Lord Jesus, and I entrust my eternal destiny fully
into His hands and to the ministry of the Holy Spirit
who has sealed my salvation.*

Once you have affirmed your salvation, pray the prayer:

> *In the name of my Lord Jesus Christ and by the
> power of His blood, I here and now renounce and dis-
> own all the ways in which I have given any ground to
> Satan and his demon powers. I ask my Lord Jesus
> Christ to evict from my life any controlling powers of
> darkness and to send them where they may never con-
> trol or trouble me again.*

THE SEVEN STEPS TO FREEDOM

As you proceed through the steps to freedom, severe demonic
assault may occur at any time. Do not allow this to happen. It will
require specific action on your part. As a manifestation begins,
use an authoritative verbal command such as the following:

> *In the name of my Lord Jesus Christ, I forbid
> any demonic manifestation that would interfere with
> this renunciation. By the power of the blood of the
> Lord Jesus Christ, I keep you subdued and unable to
> manifest in any way while I am working through this
> renunciation process.*

You are now ready to begin the seven steps.

STEP 1: RENOUNCE ALL PAST INVOLVEMENTS

Renounce all involvements with false religions, occult practices, divination, magic, sorcery, witchcraft, spiritistic healings,
séances, and similar activities (Deut. 18:9–14; Eph. 5:8–14).

Appendix 1, the Spiritual Experience Questionnaire, can assist in the search process. Do not dismiss any exposure as insignificant. The most trivial experimentation may have opened the door to harassment by the Enemy. Pray for the Lord to grant remembrance of all matters that need renunciation. Offer them frequently as you work through each step. Try this sample prayer:

> *I ask the Lord Jesus Christ to enable me to recall any and all spiritistic activities or false religious practices that have given any claim against me by the powers of darkness.*

Ask the Lord to release you from the consequences of any spiritistic involvements in which you were either a passive or active participant, and which you may have forgotten. They may include spiritistic rituals at birth or infancy, satanic ritual abuse (SRA), repressed traumatic memories (deaths, fears, injuries, physical abuse), or any spiritistic healing in which you may have participated. Carefully renounce each involvement through prayer. Use the following sample prayer:

> *Lord Jesus Christ, I confess that I may have been involved in harmful religious rituals and spiritistic practices that I no longer remember. I renounce all such forgotten involvements, and I ask You to sever any claims of darkness on me that are due to such involvement. I ask my Lord Jesus Christ to reclaim all ground Satan's kingdom may have gained in such things.*

Make a list of all those things the Holy Spirit enables you to remember that have to do with spiritistic acts or false religious rituals in which you participated. Carefully examine the list for unwitting acts of worship of demonic powers. Even the removal of your shoes at a religious shrine may have been an act of worship! Deliberately renounce each involvement on your list with a prayer like the one that follows.

> *Lord Jesus Christ, I confess that I have been involved in the false belief of [name the false system]. I ask for Your cleansing and forgiveness, and I renounce [false system] as a sinful counterfeit and a sin against true Christianity. I ask my Lord Jesus Christ to reclaim all ground Satan's kingdom is claiming against me because of my involvement.*

After prayerfully working through your list, add the following authoritative command against any controlling, harassing powers of darkness.

> *In the name of my Lord Jesus Christ and by the power of His blood, I command every wicked spirit who has assignment against me because of my false religious practices and spiritistic and occult sins to leave my presence. You and all your emissaries must go where my Lord Jesus Christ sends you.*

STEP 2: RENOUNCE ALL DECEPTIONS

Begin this step with a renunciation of all lying that has been a part of your life. This includes all deliberate lies, half-truths, and other deceptive practices. Lying is Satan's native language, and those who resort to his ways open themselves to his control. Ask the Lord to reveal all your deceptive ways to mind. Since lying is a sin of the flesh, use the procedure we presented in chapter 6.

Renounce the lies you have believed and have put into action. This is an area in which Christians are particularly vulnerable. To believe a lie of the Enemy and to act on it is to open the door to Satan's subtle control. Ask yourself the following questions:

- Have I accepted an unbiblical view of my self-worth?
- Am I holding judgmental or negative views toward fellow believers?
- Do I question or doubt God's love and goodness?
- Are any fears controlling me?
- How do I give expression to those fears?

Another aspect of renunciation is the development of a series of daily disciplines that will align yourself with God's truth. Become devoted to the following daily disciplines:

- Memorize God's Word, since it is the Word of Truth (John 17:17).
- Meditate on the Person of Truth, our Lord Jesus Christ, as well as His finished work (John 14:6).
- Prevailing prayer facilitates this discipline (John 14:6).
- Ponder the Holy Spirit's ministries. He is the Spirit of Truth (John 14:17; 15:26; 16:13).
- Regularly attend and participate in a local church that values and teaches God's Word. It is the "pillar and foundation of truth" (1 Tim. 3:15).

Reclaim the ground you yielded through the practice of lying or believing Satan's deceptions. Pray in this manner:

Loving Lord Jesus, I recognize that I've been deceived by practicing and believing in Satan's native language. I specifically renounce my participation in [name lie or action], and I ask that the blood of Jesus Christ would cleanse me of this wicked insult to Your truth. I ask that my Lord Jesus Christ would reclaim any and all ground Satan's kingdom is claiming against me because of my participation in this lie.

After you cover all the areas of lying on your list, use an authoritative summary command of resistance. I recommend the following prayer:

> *In the name of my Lord Jesus Christ and by the power of His blood, I command every wicked spirit assigned against me because of my telling and believing lies to leave my presence. You and all of your emissaries must leave and go where the Lord Jesus Christ sends you.*

STEP 3: REMOVE ALL BITTERNESS

Begin this step with the recognition that a Christian's refusal to forgive another who has wronged him is a serious matter. A lack of forgiveness gives Satan an opportunity to take advantage of a Christian (2 Cor. 2:10–11). Satan is a schemer, a manipulator, and a crafty opponent who takes advantage of every chance to bring believers under his control.

The apostle Paul identified in 2 Corinthians 2:10–11 that a lack of forgiveness is one of Satan's devices to penetrate a believer's protection. A lack of forgiveness may cause God to discipline a believer by allowing tormenting demonic activity as a corrective instrument in that believer's life. (See Matt. 18:21–25, 32–35.)

Jesus told the parable of the unforgiving servant (Matt. 18:21–35) to emphasize the urgency of a believer to forgive another's sins even up to "seventy times seven" times (v. 22 NKJV). Such enormous forgiveness reflects the level God extended toward us when He saved us. It was undeserved and unearned in any way.

In the parable, the master disciplines his unforgiving servant by turning him over to the "torturers" to suffer discipline. Who are these torturers? The Greek word for torturers (*basanistees*) is the same root word Peter used to describe what happened to Lot as a result of his sojourn into Sodom (2 Peter 2:7–9). Lot's torment as a righteous man by the careless ways he was living in Sodom was the same kind the master unleashed against his unforgiving servant in Jesus' parable. This represents corrective discipline, not wrath. I suspect the torturers are a reference to God's allowing demons to harass and torment a forgiven believer who refuses to forgive. The torment remains until the unforgiving one learns to lay aside his bitterness and forgive just as he was forgiven.

Forgiveness of others is a basic cornerstone of God's expectations of those who have received God's forgiveness. Paul wrote in Colossians 3:13 that we are to forgive others in the same way God forgave us. A refusal to forgive disrupts our fellowship with the Lord and circumvents His blessings until we resolve the issue of forgiveness. It's that important to our heavenly Father.

Often the progress of a believer in getting to know the Lord is put on hold until the believer deals with his unforgiving heart. Sometimes it takes time to work through the brutalizing hurts of life before forgiveness is realized, but it is essential that it come. Even sexual abuse by a parent or grandparent must be resolved through forgiveness before freedom and peace can come to a wounded person. Since unforgiveness is our attempt to punish the offender, we are usurping from God what He has reserved for Himself. (See Rom. 12:17–21.)

Recognize that forgiveness requires deliberate, willed action. Forgiveness must be based on Christ's finished work that removes every sin from the believer's record. (See Ps.

103:10–12; Col. 2:15.) Forgiveness must be a choice of the will: a conscious decision to let the offender off the hook and by that choice to free oneself from the past. Forgiveness must recognize the truth of your own hurt and another's wrong. Once recognized, a decision must be made to forgive and to leave the matter totally to God. Learn to practice forgiveness. Begin by preparing a list of everyone who has offended or hurt you in your lifetime. Ask the Lord to help you remember each one you need to remember. You may need to include God and even yourself in this list. You may find it beneficial to write out a careful description of the offense. Be honest and express how you feel. An additional helpful resource is Neil T. Anderson's twelve steps to forgiveness that he includes in his book *Victory over the Darkness.*

Next, say a prayer of forgiveness and renunciation of your bitterness toward each person and incident on your list. Pray a prayer like this:

> *Lord Jesus Christ, I've sinned against You and my heavenly Father by harboring resentment, hurt, and bitterness against [name of person] for his/her offense against me. Please cleanse me of this wickedness, and I now unconditionally forgive [name] for that wrong, just as You forgave me all my sins.*

After you've prayed through your list, it is wise to exercise your authority over intrusive demonic activity in prayer. I recommend the following:

> *I ask my Lord Jesus Christ to reclaim all ground in my life that Satan's kingdom has claimed against me because of my unforgiveness and bitterness. In the name of my Lord Jesus Christ and by the power of*

*His blood, I command all powers of darkness assigned
against me because of my unforgiving ways to leave
my presence! You must go where my Lord Jesus
Christ sends you. I submit myself only to the controlling and indwelling work of the Holy Spirit.*

STEP 4: RENOUNCE ALL REBELLION AGAINST GOD

Rebellion is as the sin of witchcraft in the eyes of our holy
God, and 1 Samuel 15:22–23 clearly indicates how seriously
God views any rebellious rejection of His directive will.

Ask the Lord to reveal to you all expressions of your
rebellion against His authority in your life, including the
following:

- God's activity in your life
- God's call on your life
- All areas of willful disobedience
- All areas of complaint and disappointment
- Rebellion involving the rejection of God-ordained
  authority over you
- Civil government (Rom. 13:1–5; 1 Peter 2:13–17)
- Parents (Eph. 6:1–3)
- Husband or wife (Eph. 5:25–30; 1 Peter 3:1–2)
- Employer (Eph. 6:5–9; 1 Peter 2:18–21)
- Church leaders (Heb. 13:17)

Now renounce each specific act of rebellion on your list.
Here is a recommended prayer:

*Loving heavenly Father, I confess that my sin
of [name offense] is as the sin of witchcraft before
Your holy eyes. I ask the Lord Jesus Christ to
reclaim all ground I've given to Satan's kingdom
by this rebellion and to cleanse me by His blood*

*from all the soil of my rebellious sin. May the Holy
Spirit grant to me the fruit of His submissive control
over my mind, will, emotions, and body.*

Evict any controlling spirits of rebellion with a command
of this nature:

> *In the name of my Lord Jesus Christ and by the
> power of His blood, I command all rebellious demonic
> powers seeking to rule over me because of my rebellious
> practices to leave my presence. You and all your emis-
> saries must go where my Lord Jesus Christ sends you.*

STEP 5: RECOGNIZE AND RENOUNCE EXPRESSIONS OF PRIDE

It is important to deal with pride because pride was at the
core of Satan's fall. He wanted to be like God. (See Isa.
14:11–14; Ezek. 28:1–19.) Pride on our part is our attempt to
claim for ourselves what belongs only to God. (See James
4:6–10; 1 Peter 5:1–10.) The cure for pride is to ask God to
grant us a humble heart. But before God can grant that to us,
we need to identify all the ways sinful pride is finding expression in our life. That's right, we need to make another list.
Pray for the Holy Spirit to bring to mind every example of
pride and write it down. Confess and renounce these sinful
expressions of pride through a prayer of this type:

> *In the name of my Lord Jesus Christ, I renounce
> and confess the sin of my prideful [name offense]. I
> ask my Lord Jesus Christ to reclaim the ground this
> pride has given to Satan's kingdom. May the precious
> blood of my Lord Jesus Christ wash me clean from
> the soil of this sinful pride. I ask my Lord to grant to
> me the grace of a yielded, humble heart before Him. I
> here and now resist all prideful demonic attempts to*

rule over me in any way. In the name of my Lord
Jesus Christ, I command all prideful spirits and all
their emissaries to leave me and to go where my Lord
Jesus Christ sends them.

STEP 6: RENOUNCE SINS OF THE FLESH

Persistent patterns of sin, or "besetting sin," have the ability to hold us back from growing in the Lord. Read Galatians 5:19–21 and do the following:

◻ Make a list of the besetting, fleshly sins that have in the past or are now ruling and controlling you. Recognize that the continual practice of fleshly sins gives ground to the Devil.

◻ List all the partners with whom you've been sexually immoral. Then confess and renounce these unions in a prayer such as the following:

> *I confess and renounce my sinful sexual union with*
> *[name of person or persons] as a sin against God and*
> *my own body. I ask the cleansing blood of my Lord*
> *Jesus Christ to free me from the guilt and ground I've*
> *given by my sexual union with _____. I renounce*
> *all bonding with _____ that took place in the sex-*
> *ual act, and I ask You to free me from the consequences*
> *of that bonding. I renounce all wicked spirits that have*
> *a claim against me because of that sexual sin. In the*
> *name of my Lord Jesus Christ, I break and renounce*
> *all transfer claims. I ask the Lord Jesus Christ to send*
> *any and all transferred powers of darkness to where He*
> *wants them to go.*

◻ Confess and renounce in a deliberate manner the ground you have given to the Adversary by habitually yielding to these besetting sins. Use the following sample prayer:

> *I confess and renounce my repeated yielding to my besetting sin of [name the sin] as an act that gives ground or place for the rule of unclean spirits in my life. I ask that the blood of my Lord Jesus Christ would wash me clean from the soil and power of this besetting sin. I ask that my Lord Jesus Christ would reclaim all the ground that I've given by this habitual sin. In the name of my Lord Jesus Christ and by the power of His blood, I command the unclean spirit of [name besetting sin] and all of his emissaries to leave my presence. You must now go where my Lord Jesus Christ sends you.*

STEP 7: RENOUNCE THE CLAIMS OF DARKNESS THROUGH GENERATIONAL TRANSFER

It is important to renounce the claims the Adversary has against you due to the sins of your ancestors. Begin with a careful study of the biblical passages in this book that deal with generational transfer. You may also want to reread chapter 2, "The Principle of Generational Transfer."

Perform a deliberate renunciation of all generational claims by the Adversary. This will require prayerful and tactful research. We may be able to do so simply by noting the obvious defeats that were visible in our parents' and grandparents' lives. But we may also need to engage in conversations with living family members to discover other strongholds that may be beyond our observation. It is, of course, helpful to make a list of those things that may suggest the presence of strongholds that existed in our generational lineage. Do this for each side of your family history. Make a list for your mother's side of the family and another for your father's side of the family.

The lists may include practices or behavioral traits that range from the occult to alcoholism, pornography, and gambling addictions. They may also include emotional responses and practices. Name all the specific areas where there appears to be evidence of possible generational strongholds. A biblical renunciation pattern may consist of the following:

> *Through the power of the precious blood of my Lord Jesus Christ, I affirm that I have been redeemed from all consequences of the empty way of life handed down to me and my family through the sins and failures of my forefathers on my father's side of the family. I specifically renounce strongholds of [name possible areas]. In the name of my Lord Jesus Christ, I forbid any powers of darkness from controlling me or the family members for whom I am responsible because of ground given by my father's generational lineage that extends back three and four generations. I renounce such claim. I claim the death, burial, and resurrection of my Lord Jesus Christ as fully sufficient to release and set me and my family free from all generational transfer claims by the powers of darkness.*

After dealing with any generational claim by the powers against your father's side of the family, exercise the same care to deal with your generational heritage on your mother's side of the family. Include stepparents and adoptive parents in this exercise. If any of your immediate family members are living a lifestyle that gives ground to the Enemy, a continuing renunciation of transfer claim is necessary. If any member of your family is involved in occult activity, a prayer similar to the one above will be helpful.

The aforementioned renunciations provide an excellent resource for use by the parents of adopted children. Their biological siblings, parents, grandparents, and others may be giving ground to the work of Satan's kingdom. Adoptive parents have the responsibility and spiritual authority to exercise protective care over their children.

THE POWER OF RENUNCIATION PRAYER

After you have worked through the steps to freedom, it is good to spend time in prayer, waiting before the Lord. The sincere confessions, renunciations, and assertions of the believer's authority over darkness will strengthen the believer as well as weaken the assaulting powers of darkness. For many the release and freedom will be obvious and immediate.

"I've never felt so clean and free," stated a medical doctor after he worked through the steps. "I only wish someone had helped me years ago to go through these steps."

A college student compared her final year of school to her previous year. Her release was dramatic. "I never realized I was under so much stress and bondage from the Evil One. I had put all the blame on myself. Now that I'm free, I can see how deceived I was."

A businessman who had difficulty working through the renunciation of besetting sins because of past promiscuity found a marvelous renewal in his marriage and family relationships. As he renounced the inappropriate bonding that had resulted from his past sexual sins, fierce opposition had come against him in the form of confusion and spiritual oppression. We had to stop several times and command the interference to cease. "I see my relationship to my wife in an entirely new frame of reference," he declared months later. "I never believed something as basic as the freedom steps could so totally transform our marriage."

With a joyful smile his wife confirmed his remarks. "I not only have back the husband I married," she told me, "but he is more thoughtful, considerate, and supportive than I ever dreamed he could be."

These steps have significantly helped many to claim their freedom. At some point I always seek to lead my counselees through these important steps. And in some cases we have had to repeat the process several times before any healing could take place.

After you have completed the steps to freedom, pray a wrap-up prayer similar to the one in appendix 4. The prayer is useful anytime one senses the need for it. It's another tool one can use to yield once again to the sanctifying work of the Holy Spirit. Feel free to copy it and keep it handy. Regardless of your place in life, you can benefit from the seven steps to freedom I have presented. Your children, too, will experience great benefit, since you will have strength to help them grow to where they can confidently confront the Adversary.

Prayer That Defeats the Rule of Evil

Sally Graham, a supervisor in a Midwest manufacturing plant, has lived in America's heartland for almost twenty-five years. More important, she is a veteran of warfare praying, both for herself and her children. Each of her three children, even prior to their births, has benefited from her watchful prayers. For the benefit of other parents who are just learning about warfare praying, I asked Sally to describe some of her experiences from many years of prayerful watch.

THE GRAHAMS' SPIRITUAL BATTLES

At the time of this writing, her two sons, Kevin and Steve, are ages ten and sixteen, respectively. Kelly, her only daughter, is nineteen. Sally agreed to share with you an incident of spiritual warfare from each child's life. Parenting demands spiritual insights and consistent application of spiritual principles. These three accounts remind us that as parents we face serious battles in the rearing of our children in a world where the Adversary prowls.

Kevin's Story

"Mommy, every time you turn out the light and leave my room, I see a face on my ceiling!" Kevin was clutching my hand and whispering to me. His frightened, intense voice was at a level just above a whisper. I knew my seven-year-old was really spooked. He was afraid! The sinister face that appeared on the ceiling with its threatening sneer had unnerved my youngest child. As he told me, I felt a familiar chill that I had experienced before. Such spiritual powers are very real and they want us to be afraid.

I considered myself a spiritual warfare veteran. I'd experienced twenty-five years of exercising daily, active warfare praying over my own life and the lives of friends and family members. Kevin was my third child, and although this was his first experience with the appearance of a face, we'd weathered several other encounters with supernatural evil. I knew how to deal with a matter like this. I was mindful to reassure Kevin by my measured calm that he didn't have to be afraid.

"Kevin, we can take care of that problem right now!" I assured my son. "The face you see is there because Satan's kingdom wants to rule you by fear. But we have the Lord Jesus Christ on our side and we can make this stop." I took him into my arms. My approach quieted and greatly reassured him that his Lord was in charge. I then began to pray aloud with bold confidence.

> *In the name of the Lord Jesus Christ and by the power of His blood, I bind all workings of Satan or any of his kingdom who are putting faces on the ceiling to frighten Kevin. I command these wicked powers to leave our house, our family, and Kevin's mind and room. You must go to the place the Lord Jesus Christ sends you. As a Christian united with*

my Lord Jesus Christ, as a priest of the living and
true God, and as Kevin's protecting mother, I forbid
these wicked powers to work in our home again in
any way. I ask our heavenly Father to station His
holy angels in Kevin's room to ensure the end of these
evil intrusions.

As I finished my prayer, Kevin hugged me appreciatively. I returned his hug and gave him a mother's loving kiss. "You don't have to be afraid, Kevin. Mommy's not afraid of any old faces the Devil tries to use to scare us. If that ever happens again, you command it to leave with a prayer like this: 'In the name of the Lord Jesus Christ, leave my room right now!' If they don't leave immediately, then you come and get me and I'll pray again so you can go back to sleep."

He nodded in agreement, but I could sense Kevin's apprehension over those ending words. He wasn't interested in having to handle any more encounters with faces. His confidence was building, however, and he did need to resist on his own. His dad and I prayed over his room with him before we turned off the lights, but even then the apparitions tried to return. Kevin began to resist with his own heart and authority. The faces disappeared and have never returned.

My husband, Charlie, and I grew up in a generation of Christian parents and grandparents who did not understand spiritual warfare. Charlie had seen apparitions in the form of snakes on his bedroom walls when he was a child. He cried about it and complained several times to his parents, but because his parents lacked training and a biblical perspective, they didn't hold a clue as to what was happening to Charlie. They used the rational, logical approach: "Charlie, there are absolutely no snakes on the walls of your room! Now you just forget about such nonsense!"

Of course, Charlie's parents were right. Real snakes were not crawling on Charlie's walls. Nevertheless, Charlie was seeing something very real. The inability to recognize the battle and the failure to use the available tools to make the apparitions cease not only harmed my husband but also left the door open for the harassment of our son. That's a spiritual tragedy.

I praise the Lord that He is opening the eyes of many Christian parents in this generation. He is opening our eyes not only to the reality of physical and spiritual opposition from spirit beings, He is also showing us His power to stop these attacks. Charlie's parents have come to understand spiritual warfare and to join us in praying for their grandchildren. That's brought an added dimension of power.

Three years after I prayed on Kevin's behalf, he said to one of his grandparents, "I just couldn't live a single day without my Lord! He helps me in everything I have to do!" Kevin is definitely all boy, but he is growing to love and appreciate how necessary and powerful Jesus is. That's the greatest lesson he will ever learn.

If you suspect that your child may be experiencing a spiritual attack of some kind, don't let your fears cause you to doubt the Lord's goodness. God does have your best interests and those of your child in mind, but Satan would have us believe otherwise. Do not give in to Satan's lies, but rather boldly use the tools and weapons of warfare God has made available. You will then see the attacks cease, and the reality of your faith in the power of Christ will take hold. Like Kevin, we all have to learn that we "just can't live a single day without our Lord!"

STEVE'S STORY

My older son, Steve, and I shared a special bond up until his twelfth year. At that time I started to feel the normal pain of my child's growing up as Steve started to withdraw from me.

I'd observed most of the boys I've known go through difficult behavior patterns as they progressed through puberty. For that reason, I was not too threatened by his turning away. I thought he was merely cutting the apron strings in keeping with the hormonal changes boys his age go through. Though it hurt to see my little boy growing up, I took it all pretty much in stride.

As we entered the second year of so-called normal adolescent resistance and irritability, I noted a subtle shift in Steve's attitudes toward me. What I had accepted as an immature lack of tolerance and impatient annoyance now included fierce anger and even emotions of hatred. Instead of simply challenging my views with his own contrary thinking, Steve began to taunt me and ridicule my opinions. When he was around me, he set himself up as the final authority on every issue. I knew we had moved from a normal growth pattern to a danger zone of rebellion. I became quite concerned.

I didn't handle Steve's growing challenge to my parental authority well at all. I was becoming more and more emotionally distraught. The verbal badgering, the scornful looks, and the lack of respect were extremely threatening to me. I was feeling considerable anger. I was not about to let my son rule me or run his own life at thirteen years of age. My whole perspective of biblical principles caused me to justify my responses to my son's challenge. I handled the problem very badly.

I began to fight the battle with lectures and shouting. Every time Steve would write me off or shut me out, I would foster feelings of resentment. I began to cook emotionally. The pressure cooker was really building up steam. Finally the pot boiled over. Steve and I fell into a screaming, shouting, and shoving encounter that left us both exhausted and weeping. A depressed sense of parental failure now joined my resentment and anger.

The explosive trauma did stop my destructive responses to a very serious problem. I began to see spiritual truth again.

Though I thought of myself as a "warfare mom," I had to admit I had not seen this battle from a spiritual perspective. My pastor-counselor helped both Steve and me to regain some perspective. We needed to fight the right enemy and to use weapons of warfare to help us properly relate.

As soon as I could, I spent some time alone in my Lord's presence, repenting of my wrong responses to my son. I sensed the need for warfare prayer against what the Enemy was doing to my relationship with Steve. With tearful but now righteous anger, I was able to pray aggressively.

> *In the name of the Lord Jesus Christ and by the power of His blood, I pull down the walls, relationships, and barriers that Satan and his kingdom are building between Steve and me. I ask the Lord Jesus Christ to demolish all the destructive strongholds the kingdom of darkness has been able to erect between us. I ask my Lord to unleash the mighty power of the loving heavenly Father on our relationship to make it all You want it to be. I ask the Holy Spirit to put within Steve and me God's fruit of love, joy, peace, patience, kindness, goodness, faithfulness, gentleness, and self-control. By faith, I pray the healing power of the true and living God on our broken relationship that we might glorify Your name.*

In that quiet time alone with the Lord, I also prayed for the wisdom to know how to reach my son. I knew my anger and resentment had deeply wounded him. I felt so ashamed. Satan even wanted to use my guilt to stop my move toward victory, but I would have none of that. The Lord began to give me immediate insights. I needed to apologize and ask Steve's forgiveness for my wrong responses to his needs. He also gave me insights about verbalizing my admiration for Steve and the talents God had put into him. He needed the ministry of his mom's encouragement now more than ever.

The Lord also showed me that in my hurt toward Steve, I had abandoned all physical gestures toward my son that communicate caring love. I knew I had to be more mature now and not treat him as a little boy, but physical gestures that communicate love were desperately important to rebuild the brokenness between us. At first it was difficult. Even a hand on the shoulder elicited stiff, rigid body language. But it did not deter me. I ignored his unreturned hugs. By faith I kept reaching out to him with physical gestures. A light tap on the shoulder as I commended some aspect of his growing manhood, a squeeze of his arm, even an occasional tousling of his hair began to communicate. The hugs and quick kisses as we parted were a part of God's rebuilding tools. One day I saw a flickering smile of appreciation on his face; that was the beginning of Steve's ability to return my gestures with hugs of his own. We were on our way.

Verbal commendations and physical gestures of caring love were very important to the healing of our broken relationship. Within a week, the tensions were fading. Within the first month, I was confident that we were out of the danger zone. Warfare praying began to destroy the spiritual walls of hostility and hatred that darkness had been building. That encouraged me to intensify my intercession.

We've come a long way since those dark days of defeat. I feel we have reached a better-than-normal relationship. Now sixteen and six feet tall, Steve has a deep bass voice. His almost fully developed, adult body has moved beyond much of the hormonal craziness we once faced. He's becoming a godly man. I'm so thankful! Grace really is unmerited favor and is working even when we blow it. I know warfare prayer made the difference. Without the use of those "weapons of warfare" the Lord Jesus Christ won for us on the cross and in His resurrection, I'm certain our relationship would still be in crisis and getting worse by the day. Disaster would have overtaken us. Thank You, Lord Jesus Christ, for Your rescue!

KELLY'S STORY

From my biased perspective, Kelly has been the perfect daughter from the day she was born. I called her my "warfare baby." As she lay in her crib each night, I would stand there in the shadows of her room and pray the Ephesians 6 spiritual armor onto her. I often think in pictures, and I could visualize each tiny piece of specially designed baby armor fitting into place on her little person.

> *In the name of the Lord Jesus Christ and by the power of His blood, I put the full armor of God on Kelly Christian Graham. I place on her the belt of truth, the breastplate of righteousness, the sandals of peace, the shield of faith, the helmet of salvation, and the sword of the Spirit. I place on her and all around her the covering of the precious blood of the Lord Jesus Christ and the protection of prayer. I ask my heavenly Father to assign holy angels to watch over her and protect her. I invite the Holy Spirit to minister to every part of her being. Bring her to Christ when she's old enough to understand, and fill her with love, joy, peace, patience, kindness, goodness, faithfulness, gentleness, and self-control from infancy on. I ask You, dear heavenly Father, to make Kelly everything You desire her to be.*

If I could better relate to you how wonderfully the Lord answered those prayers, you would find it difficult to believe. Though she gave evidence of the fallen nature we all receive from our first parents, to me she was a dream child come true. Now nineteen, she's in her second year at a Christian college, where she has enjoyed dating several young men. This is important because her dating life in high school was so bleak it was almost nonexistent. I'm almost ashamed to admit that Kelly's "warfare mom" did not recognize the spiritual nature of her dating problems until after severe emotional damage had already taken place.

Kelly had many friends in both school and church. Her personality, long blonde hair, and hourglass figure enabled her to be chosen as a cheerleader. Yet, unbelievable as it sounds, she had never been asked out for a date. At first she laughed it off, but eventually it got to her.

As her junior year began, Kelly decided at the urging of one of her best friends to stop feeling sorry for herself about her dateless life. She should take matters into her own hands and ask one of her Christian male friends to take her to homecoming. It would just be a friendship night out where she could at least get in on some of the social fun.

Kelly first called Tom. She'd enjoyed several study times with Tom when he'd come over to the house for the evening. Tom turned her down cold. Even worse was that he concluded that Kelly had a crush on him and he changed his whole attitude toward her. He avoided her. He wouldn't speak to her or even look her way for several months.

She asked Jim next. They had been good friends since the fifth grade. Though not attracted to him in any romantic way, she liked his sense of humor and quiet friendliness. Jim, too, said no without any explanation. Their friendly relationship also seemed to be fractured after that.

Kelly was shattered. The humiliation of asking and being refused was almost unbearable. "What is wrong with me? Why do boys hate me?" Her hurtful wail almost broke my heart. Yet, I didn't know what to say.

As girlfriend after girlfriend went on date after date, Kelly began to withdraw. I gave my speeches about trusting God with your life. In a desperate attempt to be helpful, I mumbled out one day, "Maybe God wants you to be single, honey. You have to be open to His perfect will for your life." That was a real zinger. My pious platitude only added to Kelly's dirge of despair. She was hurt, disappointed, and hopelessly empty. What aroused my righteous anger was the lie I could see building in Kelly's mind and emotions. She was seeing herself as ugly and undesirable. A false perception of her true worth was pressing in on her because of her dating circumstances.

When Kelly was just a small child, Charlie and I had decided we would only allow her to date Christians when she was old enough for that social life. We explained that to her as she neared the proper age for dating, and Kelly accepted the restriction without question. She saw the biblical principle of warning against an unequal yoke and was glad for the guidance of her parents. The large youth program of our church provided many opportunities for social interaction with Christian young men. I just couldn't understand what was wrong. Were these Christian boys blind or what?

As Kelly began her senior year, I wondered if she would face another dateless year. I finally began to feel some spiritual concern. As I saw the deep wounds she was experiencing over this issue, I decided to lay it before the Lord. I was concerned about her deepening depression, and I could do nothing to help her with my words and advice. I also felt that she had patiently waited long enough. If it was God's plan for Kelly to remain single, that was completely acceptable to me, but Kelly needed spiritual help. She needed to be rid of her "I'm a reject" self-image. It was building destructive patterns into her life that caused me deep concern.

I decided to fast and pray over Kelly's dating life for three days. As I started into the second day of the fast, I was feeling less than enthusiastic, and besides that, I was extremely hungry. Kelly had snapped out of the depression and seemed resigned to the fact that she would not have a date to homecoming again this year. I was about to break my fast but thought it best to seek the Lord's approval before making such a decision. I started to pray, "Lord, You know I am very hungry. Please let me break this fast now if it isn't accomplishing Your will. I'm not only hungry, but I'm not even sure of the purpose of my fast. Please give me guidance now in a way that will confirm Your will to me."

Immediately, my mind was activated. I saw the picture of a strong, formidable-looking wall in my mind. Large, ugly, evil, sinister-looking soldiers were standing shoulder to shoulder guarding the wall. I believed this was God's insight into what was happening in Kelly's dating life. The Enemy had built strongholds of opposition and isolation around her. He was using it to destroy her sense of self-worth and ultimately to destroy her.

My devotional reading through *The One Year Bible* for that day had a message of confirmation about my vision. I could scarcely believe it as I read the passage: "Let my eyes overflow with tears night and day without ceasing; for my virgin daughter ... has suffered a grievous wound, a crushing blow" (Jer. 14:17). I wept and thanked God for His personalized message in the midst of my frustration and need.

I continued to fast and "pray without ceasing" (1 Thess. 5:17 NKJV) for the remaining days of my commitment. I feel the Lord let me see a clear picture of the crushing blow in Kelly's life and the reason for it. It was a vicious attack from the realm of darkness. I had prayed over Kelly and her future husband from the day she was born, but I had never covered her dating life with warfare prayer. Strongholds had been built with evil purposes, in part because of my failure to be watchful.

After completing the fast, I felt I needed to share with Kelly my new insights about the battle. She had a good understanding of balanced spiritual warfare and I knew she'd respond well. "Kelly, I've been unaware and insensitive to the level of pain and loss you've been experiencing over this dating issue. Though I haven't completely understood, God has. He knows exactly how you feel, and He hurts with you." I went on to share the story of my fast, my vision, and the Bible-reading text, which proved how much God knew and cared.

As I began to read the verses, Kelly buried her face in her pillow and began to weep. When she was able to compose herself, we read together *Warfare Prayer* by Dr. Victor Matthews. As we finished, Kelly breathed a deep sigh of relief and slipped quickly into a restful sleep. Her nap was short. Fifteen minutes later, the phone rang. It was for Kelly. A young man was calling to ask her to be his date to homecoming. She accepted!

My purpose in sharing this very personal account from our daughter's life is not to say that all dateless lives are caused by problems with the kingdom of darkness. Your daughter's problem might be that every boy around seems to want to date her. The issue is a watchful awareness. The destroying tactics of darkness over our children are subtle and ingenious. If you are a follower of the Lord Jesus Christ and you have given Him control of your life and the ownership of your children, you have powerful weapons to use in their defense. You can wage a winning war against the darkness seeking to rule them. Use your weapons!

Spiritual Experience Questionnaire

The first step in the seven steps to freedom outlined in chapter 10 is to renounce all involvements with false religions, occult practices, divinations, magic, sorcery, witchcraft, spiritistic healings, séances, and similar activities. The following questionnaire can help you recall those involvements, past or present, that may offer the Adversary a foothold in your life. Some of these activities can be harmless but are worth evaluating for spiritual content.

Circle Y or N as applicable.

1. Occult Exposure
   a. Have you ever visited a fortune-teller who told your fortune by cards, tea leaves, palm reading, or other means?   Y   N
   b. Do you read or follow the horoscope?   Y   N
   c. Have you ever played with games of an occult nature, such as ESP, Kabul, or others? Y   N
   d. Have you ever consulted a Ouija board/ planchette, crystal ball, tea leaves, or any other future-telling device?   Y   N

e. Have you ever had a "life" or reincarnation
   reading?   Y   N
f. Have you had your handwriting analyzed?   Y   N
g. Have you ever practiced mental or post-
   hypnotic suggestion?   Y   N
h. Have you ever cast a magic spell?   Y   N
i. Have you ever sought a psychic experience? Y   N
j. Have you ever practiced Transcendental
   Meditation (TM)?   Y   N
k. Have you ever had a "spirit guide"?   Y   N
l. Have you ever observed or participated in
   Satan worship?   Y   N
m. Have you ever been a practicing witch
   or Wiccan?   Y   N
n. Have you ever had an imaginary playmate?   Y   N
o. Does your martial arts class emphasize
   Eastern philosophy?   Y   N
p. Have you ever practiced mind control as in
   Sylon, Pathways, Zen Buddhism, etc.?   Y   N

2. Cult Involvement
   Have you ever been involved in any of the following?
      (Circle all that apply.)
      Hare Krishna
      Spiritual Frontier
      Unitarian Fellowship
      Scientology
      Latter-day Saints (Mormons)
      Jehovah's Witnesses
      Children of God
      Zen Buddhism
      Unification Church ("Moonies")
      Christian Science
      Meher Baba
      Transcendental Meditation Theosophy

Baha'i World Faith
EST/Landmark Education (addictive self-help
    seminars)
Inner Peace Movement
Rosicrucianism
Religious Research of America
The Way
Metropolitan Community Church
Kaballah
Other: _____

3. Ritual Practices, Readings, the Use of Objects
    a. Have you ever sought or participated at any time in
       healing or the treatment of disease by means of any
       of the following? (Circle all that apply.)
       Spiritualist practitioner
       Christian Science practitioner
       Pendulum healer
       Hypnosis
       Spirit healer
       Trance for diagnosis
       Psychic healer
       Other occult means: _____
    b. Have you ever received or worn an amulet,
       talisman, or charm for luck or protection?   Y   N
    c. Have you ever sought to locate missing persons
       or objects by consulting someone with psychic,
       clairvoyant, or psychometric powers?   Y   N
    d. Have you ever participated in *I Ching*?   Y   N
    e. Have you practiced or participated in "water
       witching" (dowsing or divining) to locate
       water?   Y   N
    f. Do you read or possess occult or spiritualist
       literature such as books on astrology, fortune-
       telling, interpretation of black-magic dreams,

ESP, religious cults, clairvoyance, or other
psychic phenomena?   Y   N

g. Have you ever experimented or practiced
ESP telepathy?   Y   N

h. Have you practiced any form of magic
ritual?   Y   N

i. Do you possess any occult or pagan religious
objects, relics, or artifacts that may have been
used in pagan religious rites or in the practice
of sorcery, magic, divination,
or spiritualism?   Y   N

4. Consciousness Problems

a. Have you ever lost your awareness of time or found
yourself in a location without knowing
how you arrived there?   Y   N

b. Have you ever experienced extreme sleepiness
during discussion of spiritual things?   Y   N

c. Have you ever demonstrated extraordinary
abilities such as ESP or telekinesis?   Y   N

d. Have you ever heard in your mind voices
that mock, intimidate, accuse, threaten, or
offer bargains?   Y   N

e. Have you ever heard a voice speaking from
you or another person that refers to himself
in the third person?   Y   N

f. Have you ever seen supernatural experiences,
such as the movement or disappearance of
objects?   Y   N

Warfare Prayers for the Protection of Our Children

Building on Sally Graham's testimony from chapter 11, I have assembled a number of helpful warfare prayers that provide patterns of prayer for parents and grandparents to use. Some of the prayers are new; others are from my previous writings. Many have found these prayers helpful in teaching them how to use their authority in Christ to resist the works of darkness.

Remember, the following prayers are not magical. It is only the eternal truth of God that forces darkness to retreat. Use them with that in mind. Feel free to customize the following prayers, expressing the same truth in terminology more familiar to you; it will be just as effective as the wording I have suggested.

PRAYER FOR THE PARENT

Pray this prayer in an attitude of confidence, not fear. If a parent communicates terror as he prays for his children, the parent neither reassures the child nor displays effective faith in God. The prayers of many Christian parents seem awkward and ineffective because of their own fears. Before you begin to pray for your child, pray first for yourself as a parent. Here is a sample prayer to combat the fear of losing a child to an injury, illness, or violence. (Insert your child's name in the blanks.)

> *Loving God and Father of our Lord Jesus Christ,*
> *I deliberately yield _____ into Your loving hands of*
> *care and protection. I uphold the victory and name of*
> *the Lord Jesus Christ over _____ as protection*
> *against the plans of darkness to harm and destroy*
> *_____. I ask You to assign holy angel protection and*
> *the sealing ministry of the Holy Spirit on _____*
> *at all times. I recognize the Enemy's effort to put on*
> *me a spirit of fear and terror of losing _____. I*
> *thank You for the love You have given to me for*
> *_____. I reject the fearful unbelief that darkness is*
> *trying to use to control me. Although I trust I will*
> *never have to face the loss of _____, I know You*
> *would supply me with the portion of grace and mercy*
> *I would need to walk with You through such a trial.*
> *Again, I deliberately yield up my children, myself,*
> *and all of our family into the care and keeping power*
> *of the true and living God.*

Single parents have special concerns for their children that often create fears. Here is a prayer for single parents who feel an extra burden for the protection of their children from demonic influences.

> *Heavenly Father, I bring the burden of my role*
> *as a single parent to You for Your wisdom, strength,*
> *and sustaining courage. I resist all efforts of darkness*
> *to put on me attitudes of resentment and self-pity that*
> *would only further harm the children and me. I ask*
> *You to guide and encourage me through Your Word. I*

reach out to You and look to You for Your provision in all my personal and family needs. I hold that victorious name of my Lord Jesus Christ over my children and me that we may walk in His provided victory each day. Assign Your holy, guarding, protecting angels to minister to us in our needs. Help me to be loving and submissive to You in everything. Help me to trust You with my future in every detail of life.

Prayer for Protection of Children at Bedtime

In the name of the Lord Jesus Christ, I commit _____'s mind, will, emotions, and body into the keeping, protective power of the Lord Jesus Christ, as well as the sealing ministry of the Holy Spirit while he/she sleeps. I bind and forbid any powers of darkness to tamper with any part of _____'s person on the conscious, subconscious, or unconscious level. Heavenly Father, assign Your protecting, holy angels to watch over _____'s person and room. Ensure that no powers of darkness intrude in any way while _____ sleeps.

Prayer against Hostility and Quarreling between Children

Lord Jesus Christ, just as You have taught us in Your Word, I know that the sinful nature loves to pick quarrels. Help me to teach my children the biblical principles of overcoming their flesh. I notice levels of hostility and fighting between them that may indicate spirit powers of darkness seeking to control _____ and _____. I pull down all intensifying

influences of darkness that are building walls, barri-
ers, and hostility between my children. In the name of
my Lord Jesus Christ, I forbid any powers of darkness
to create contention, anger, hate, and fighting
between my children. I ask that the lordship of Jesus
Christ and the ministry of the Holy Spirit would cre-
ate the loving relationships within our family that
honor You and bless our family.

PRAYER THAT ADDRESSES FASCINATION WITH VIOLENCE AND CRUELTY

In the name of my Lord Jesus Christ, I stand
against the violence and cruelty our culture promotes
through the entertainment media. I recognize the cul-
tural focus on violence as an expression of the murderous
ways of Satan's darkness. Loving heavenly Father, I
bring to You my concern for the tendency toward vio-
lence and cruelty I see in my child. In the name of my
Lord Jesus Christ and by the power of His blood, I resist
and renounce all powers of darkness seeking to rule and
control _____. I stand against them and command
them to leave and to go where the Lord Jesus Christ
commands them to go. I ask the Holy Spirit to establish
the loving gentleness of Christ in _____'s life.

PRAYER REGARDING HOSTILITY TOWARD SPIRITUAL TRUTH

Heavenly Father, I know Satan and his kingdom
stand in arrogant opposition to You and all Your ways
of righteousness and truth. When I note hostile atti-
tudes toward the things of God in _____'s life, I

know he/she is being deceived by the kingdom of darkness. I stand against the control and deception in the name of the Lord Jesus Christ. I renounce and tear down those strongholds of darkness that promote hostility to spiritual truth in _____'s life. I ask You to evict them from _____'s presence. I look to You, heavenly Father, to soften _____'s heart by the work of Your Spirit and to draw him/her to Yourself.

PRAYER THAT ADDRESSES UNWHOLESOME RELATIONSHIPS

You have told us in Your Word, heavenly Father, that "bad company corrupts good character" (1 Cor. 15:33). Because of that truth, I have deep concern for the corrupting influence I see taking place in _____'s life. In the name of my Lord Jesus Christ, I pull down all relationships between _____ and _____ that the powers of darkness are promoting. I ask the Lord Jesus Christ to sever all unwholesome bonding that is taking place between _____ and _____. I ask You to bring into _____'s life only those relationships that are Your will for _____'s spiritual development and moral integrity.

PRAYER TO CONFRONT OCCULT "GIFTS" AND SPIRITISTIC INTERESTS

Heavenly Father, I thank You for the direct warnings in Your Word against all occult and spiritistic activities. We have sought to carefully warn and protect our children against any interests in such evil things. I notice in _____'s life a magnetic fascina-

*tion with the spiritistic realm, especially as it relates
to [name the spiritistic interest]. I stand against all
powers of darkness that seek to influence and draw
_____ into these spiritistic interests. I resist them
in the name of the Lord Jesus Christ and command
them to cease their wicked influence. They must leave
and go where the Lord Jesus Christ sends them.*

PRAYER REGARDING PREOCCUPATION WITH THE OPPOSITE SEX

*Thank You, heavenly Father, that You have
already chosen a life partner for _____. I pray for
You to keep _____ for that chosen one and keep
him/her for _____. Thank You for hearing my
prayer, and I ask You to work out this relationship in
Your perfect time and way. I pray against the
unwholesome attraction toward the opposite sex that I
see developing in _____'s life. I stand against any
corrupting schemes of darkness that may be promoting this preoccupation with the opposite sex in
_____'s life. In the name of my Lord Jesus Christ, I
resist their evil work and command them to leave and
go where the Lord Jesus sends them. I ask for wisdom
and understanding to help _____ develop spiritually sensitive attitudes toward the opposite sex that
will honor and glorify You.*

PRAYER CONCERNING REBELLION AGAINST AUTHORITY

*In the name of the Lord Jesus Christ and by the
power of His blood, I come against the spirit of rebel-*

lion I see seeking to deceive and control _____. I renounce and resist that spirit of rebellion and all those like it that are influencing _____ to reject authority. I command you and your emissaries to leave, and you must go where the Lord Jesus Christ sends you. I ask that the Holy Spirit would effect within _____'s person the same submissive attitude toward authority that the Lord Jesus Christ demonstrated in His earthly life.

Prayer against Sexual Perversion

Loving heavenly Father, I thank You for Your high and holy purpose for human sexuality. I pray in the name of my Lord Jesus Christ against the perversion and misuse of this gift You have given. Through my words, prayers, and conduct, grant me the wisdom to convey to my children biblical values concerning their sexuality. In the name of my Lord Jesus Christ and by the power of His blood, I resist all strongholds of sexual perversion the Adversary has assigned to manipulate and rule over _____'s sexuality. I specifically resist strongholds of [name any inappropriate sexual tendency you have observed in your child]. I command them to cease all activity against _____. They and all their emissaries must leave and go where the Lord Jesus Christ sends them.

Prayer regarding Substance Abuse

In the name of my Lord Jesus Christ and by the power of His blood, I come against those powers of dark-

ness who seek to create and intensify _____'s dependence on [name substance] to cope with life. I renounce and reject that deception of darkness in _____'s life that has made him/her dependent on this substance. I ask the Lord Jesus Christ to expel all powers of darkness associated with _____'s bondage to the place where they can never control or manipulate him/her again. I look to the shepherding lordship of Jesus Christ to effect the release and freedom of _____. May the mighty work of the Holy Spirit remove this dependence and replace it with the joyful fruit of His full control.

PRAYER ABOUT SPIRITISTIC THEMES IN OUR CULTURE

Loving heavenly Father, I know You hate our culture's preoccupation with spiritistic themes and all that promotes supernatural evil. I cry out against it in prayer and ask You to discredit this practice and awaken our culture to reject it. Grant to me the wisdom and action to be salt and light against this darkness. Help me to warn and inform my children about the evils of these bombardments. In the name of the Lord Jesus Christ, I ask You to protect them from any harm by these influences of darkness. Grant them the wisdom to discern and reject spiritistic promotion and activity whenever they face it.

PRAYER FOR LIFE PURPOSE AND FUTURE GOALS

Thank You, heavenly Father, that "all the days ordained for me were written in your book before one of them came to be" (Ps. 139:16). I rejoice in Your good

*and satisfying plan for _____'s future. At the
moment, _____ seems to lack direction and purpose in his/her life. In the name of the Lord Jesus
Christ, I resist all efforts of darkness to obscure and
misdirect _____'s life into a purposeless future. I
ask You to sovereignly direct and reveal to _____
Your plan for him/her. Grant to him/her wisdom to
discern Your will and to enter it joyfully and obediently.*

PRAYER FOR AN OUT-OF-CONTROL CHILD

It may be wise to slip away to a private place for this intercession. At other times it may be important to take your
distraught child into your arms and to pray for him or her out
loud. The age of your child, the nature of the loss of control,
the place and time, and the past history of the problem are
factors that will influence your application of this prayer.

*In the mighty name of my Lord Jesus Christ and
by the power of His blood, I come against any and all
powers of darkness causing or intensifying the out-of-
control behavior of _____. I subdue you and all your
workers in the presence of the Lord Jesus Christ, and I
command you to cease your wicked, manipulative work
against _____. You and all your emissaries must leave
_____'s presence, and you must go where the Lord
Jesus Christ sends you. I ask You, Lord Jesus Christ, to
manifest in _____ the spiritual fruit of self-control
that comes from the Holy Spirit.*

PRAYER FOR A CHILD HEARING VOICES OR SEEING IMAGES

At times a child may hear voices or report seeing images in
the room. These may be more than mere dreams or a vivid

imagination at work. The child may be experiencing visits from spirit powers. He or she may even report having a conversation with someone in the room, even though no one is there. Here is a prayer for a child hearing voices, seeing apparitions, or having visits or conversations with spirit powers.

In the name of the Lord Jesus Christ and by the power of His blood, I bind all wicked spirits and command them to cease all activity that seeks to approach and communicate with _____. I ask You, Lord Jesus Christ, to order these intrusive powers away from _____'s presence and to confine them where they may never frighten or come near _____ again. I ask You, heavenly Father, to provide Your protecting, holy angels to guard and secure _____'s safety. Expose and destroy the evil plans of darkness that are attempting to control _____ through fear and deception. Accomplish this through the power of Your Spirit and grace. I ask this in Jesus' name and for His glory.

PRAYER FOR A CHILD'S PHOBIAS

Some fears are normal and pass with time. Others can capture a child in turmoil and fright. Such sinister fears come from the powers of darkness that are trying to dominate a child. The following is a prayer for when your child is overwhelmed by fear.

In the name of my Lord Jesus Christ, I renounce and resist all powers of darkness trying to rule over _____ by means of the fear of [name the phobia]. I pray from my position in the Lord Jesus Christ and command all strongholds of fear, along with all their

*demonic emissaries, to leave. You must go where the
Lord Jesus Christ sends you. I ask that the Holy
Spirit would replace the rule of fear with love and
peace and all the fruit of His control in _____'s life.*

Children can also pray to overcome their own fears. If
they know the Lord Jesus Christ as Savior, they can learn to
resist the Enemy. The following prayer will be helpful to train
them how to resist the Adversary.

*In the name of my Lord Jesus Christ and by the
blood He shed on the cross, I stand against all powers
of darkness trying to make me afraid of [name the
fear]. I resist you and I command all powers of fear
that are troubling me to go where the Lord Jesus
Christ sends you. I ask the Lord Jesus Christ to comfort me and to put His courage within my heart.*

PRAYER AGAINST GENERATIONAL TRANSFER
TO ADOPTED CHILDREN

Even if you have had no contact with your adopted child's
biological parents, you can help him or her resist generational
transfer by the use of the following prayer. You may want to
copy this prayer and carry it with you as a reminder of your
commitment to pray for your child.

*In the name of the Lord Jesus Christ, I praise my
heavenly Father that He has entrusted to me the care
of my adopted child, _____. I accept all responsibility
that God places on me to be a godly, protecting parent.
I ask my heavenly Father to sever all spiritual and
generational claims to _____ from the biological
family and ancestry that might bring any harmful*

influences into his/her life. I ask You to retain for
_____ *'s future benefit all generational virtues and*
blessings that would normally pass on to him/her. I ask
for and accept all the spiritual, protective, and parental
rights and responsibilities for _____.

I ask You, Lord Jesus Christ, through the power of
Your name and finished work, to sever all claims of
darkness against _____ *that are due to any genera-*
tional curses, occult rituals, or satanic covenants that
have been passed on by his/her family. I look to the sov-
ereign lordship and shepherding care of the Lord Jesus
Christ to bring _____ *to eternal salvation and to*
fulfill Your gracious will and plan for _____*'s life. I*
accept into my adopted child's life only that which comes
by way of the cross and which is in keeping with the
grace and will of the true and living God.

PRAYER FOR PROTECTION FROM ABDUCTION
OR SEXUAL ABUSE

Every child deserves this kind of protective prayer cover. Psalm
91 is there for you to claim for your child. Memorize it and daily
pray its truth over your family. Here is one prayer of protection.

Heavenly Father, we live in a very wicked
world! Only You know the awful depth of the evil
and wickedness that is before You. One of the worst
expressions of this evil is the brutal harm done to lit-
tle children by sinful people. It often ends in sexual
abuse and even the violent death of a child. Thank
You for Your hatred of this despicable evil. You warn
such an abuser that "it would be better for him to be
thrown into the sea with a large millstone tied
around his neck" (Mark 9:42). Thank You for Your

holy wrath. I ask You to stand with me, and for me, to ensure Your watchful protection against any such evil happening to _____. I have made You my dwelling and I depend on You to assign Your holy angels to _____ in constant protective care.

May the clever ploys of Satan and the wicked people he controls be unable to touch _____ in any way. Grant to me the wisdom to be alert and watchful. I acknowledge that Your sovereign, ever-present awareness is sufficient protection from this evil.

Prayer against Harmful Behavior Patterns

Heavenly Father, I see the influence of the world and fleshly desires creating a pattern of [name the problem area] within _____'s life. Grant to me the wisdom to help him/her deal with that according to the biblical patterns You set forth in Your Word. In the name of the Lord Jesus Christ and by the power of His blood, I come against any spirit powers of darkness that are seeking to control and promote evil patterns within _____'s life. I command any spirit of [name chief symptom] and all of your emissaries to cease this wicked work against _____, and you and your emissaries must leave _____ and go where the Lord Jesus Christ sends you.

Prayer for the Ability to Accept Limitations or Disabilities

If your child has a physical or mental disability, he may feel bitterness or even despair because of his limitations. One way you can encourage and protect your child during his development is to pray for him.

> *Dear heavenly Father, I thank You for*
> *_____. I also thank You for the limitations You*
> *have sovereignly placed in his/her life. Provide me*
> *with wisdom, compassion, and care in all the ways I*
> *relate to _____. In the name of the Lord Jesus*
> *Christ and by the power of His blood, I come against*
> *any powers of darkness that are seeking to create*
> *resentment, despair, and bitterness within _____'s*
> *heart because of his/her limitations. I renounce and*
> *resist all such efforts and I command them and all*
> *their emissaries to leave _____'s presence, and they*
> *must go where the Lord Jesus Christ sends them. I*
> *ask You to draw _____ into such a personal, loving*
> *relationship with You that _____ will be able to use*
> *his/her limitations in ways that will glorify God and*
> *encourage others.*

A Sample Prayer for the Protection of Children against Demonic Harassment

The following prayer can help parents who sense powers of darkness may be harassing their children. I recommend proper preparation, including fasting and personal prayer, before a parent uses this prayer on behalf of a child. Jesus warned us that replacement demonic powers can invade a person once other powers have left (Matt. 12:43–45); therefore, this prayer contains a call to "bind all other evil spirits who work with" any particular demonic influence, including "replacement" powers of darkness. It also bans the "restructuring, regrouping, or multiplying" of the activity of the powers of darkness.

> *Loving heavenly Father, I welcome Your protective presence in this time of prayer. I ask You to assign Your holy angels to protect and guard us and our children during this time of prayer.*
>
> *In the mighty name of our Lord Jesus Christ and by the power of His blood, I command all powers of darkness that have no assignment against us or our family to leave our presence. They may not intrude or*

*in any way seek to disrupt this confrontation against
those that presently seek to afflict and control
_____. I also ask that all powers of darkness that
Satan has assigned to rule over _____ be subdued
and forbidden to work in any way against _____
while he/she sleeps.*

*Thank You, Lord Jesus Christ, for Your promise
never to leave us or forsake us. I welcome Your unseen
presence with us here in this room. It's in Your
mighty name, Lord Jesus Christ, that I take authority over the forces of darkness that seek to harass and
rule over my child. As the spiritual and parental
guardian of _____, and as one who is seated with
You in the heavenly realms, I use my authority in
Christ to bind, here in the presence of the Lord Jesus
Christ, all powers of darkness that seek to control
_____.*

At this point refer to your prepared list of suspected evil
activities. Use the name of the symptom you see to identify
the suspected strongholds. They and your Lord know their
identity. Proceed with this kind of prayer.

*I pull in and bind before the Lord Jesus Christ all
powers of darkness working against _____ in
the strongholds of [name the strongholds you believe
are troubling your child: fear, hate, lust, rage, etc.]. I
command that they become and remain whole spirits.
I bind all their demonic emissaries, all backup systems, and replacement powers of darkness. There may
be no restructuring, regrouping, or multiplying of the
activity of the powers of darkness assigned against
_____. In the name of my Lord Jesus Christ and
by the power of His blood, I command these powers of*

darkness to give full attention to what my Lord Jesus Christ will say to you.

I now ask You, Lord Jesus Christ, in that spiritual realm where You dwell with me and where these powers of darkness know Your presence, to tell these scheming, troubling forces of evil where they must go. I want them to utterly and completely leave our family. I ask You to ensure that they go where they cannot return to continue their evil work.

Pause and wait for the Lord to address His will and authority over the evil forces.

I now ask that the Holy Spirit evict from _____'s presence all these powers of darkness. They must go where the Lord Jesus Christ has commanded them to go. I ask the Holy Spirit to make a thorough search in and around to make sure that there are no lingering forces of evil to deceive and rule over _____. May the Holy Spirit sanctify _____'s whole person from the defiling works of darkness. I invite the Lord Jesus Christ by the power of the Holy Spirit to do Your great work of drawing _____ to Yourself for blessings and spiritual growth.

Thank You, loving heavenly Father, for the faith and grace You have given to me to use my authority in Christ to stand in watchful protection over _____. I yield fully to Your plan and purpose for this battle. Grant to me the wisdom and grace to protect my family and to guide each one into Your plan and will. I worship You and give You thanks in the name of my Lord Jesus Christ. Amen.

APPENDIX 4

A Sample Prayer of Resistance

It's wise to use this wrap-up prayer after going through the steps to freedom. It can help those dealing with generational transfer and other issues of demonic influence to effectively resist the Devil. During counseling I sometimes ask the counselee to repeat the prayer phrase by phrase as I recite it. Regardless of how you or another person recites this prayer, understand that neither the words themselves nor a person's title or position is responsible for the freedom that one gains. The effectiveness of this prayer rests in the believer's authority to claim his or her freedom in Christ. You are welcome to copy this prayer to keep it convenient for use.

> *I worship and honor my heavenly Father, the Lord Jesus Christ, and the Holy Spirit, the true and living God who promised, "I will never leave you or forsake you." I welcome and honor the unseen presence of my Lord Jesus Christ, who promised always to be with us when we meet in His name. I honor and thank You, Lord Jesus Christ, for Your invisible presence in this very place with us. I ask You to be in*

charge and to effect only Your will and plan in our lives. I yield fully to Your will in the eviction of any and all wicked spirits from my life. I desire the Holy Spirit to do the sanctifying work within my whole person that He is there to accomplish. I ask You, Lord Jesus Christ, to assign Your holy angels to protect us from any strategies of darkness that would oppose this prayer for freedom. Keep Satan and all his opposing emissaries of evil away from us. I also ask You to ensure that the wicked spirits evicted from my presence will depart quickly and directly to the place to which You consign them.

In the name of my Lord Jesus Christ and by the power of His blood, I affirm my authority over all wicked spirits assigned to control me and hinder my life and my witness for Christ. I command all lingering wicked spirits assigned to harass, rule, and control me to cease their work and to be bound in the presence of the Lord Jesus Christ. I bind all backup systems and replacement spirits assigned to rebuild evicted strongholds. They may not do so! I command all those spirits assigned against me to be and remain whole spirits. I forbid any dividing, restructuring, or multiplying of a wicked spirit working against me. There is to be one-way movement of evil-spirit activity out of my life to the place where the Lord Jesus Christ consigns it. I pull in from other family members all those wicked spirits working under the chain of authority established by the powers of darkness assigned to rule over me. I command them all to be bound together here in the presence of my Lord Jesus Christ in that spiritual realm where He dwells with me and they know His presence. It is my will that all powers of darkness having assignment against me must hear

*and obey Him who is the Creator and Conqueror. I
command their full attention to the Lord Jesus
Christ. I declare Him to be my Redeemer and Lord. I
affirm that God has seated me with Christ Jesus in
the heavenly realms far above all principalities and
supernatural powers of darkness and evil.*

*Lord Jesus Christ, I ask You to tell all these pow-
ers of darkness assigned to afflict and rule over me
where they must go. I want them out of my life and
confined where they can never trouble me again. I
yield fully to Your sovereign plan for my life and all
of the purposes You have in this battle I have been
facing. I ask You, Lord Jesus Christ, to tell them
clearly where they must go.*

Pause briefly to honor the Lord Jesus Christ's work as He
addresses His authority and victory against the powers of
darkness who stand bound in divine accountability before
Him.

*I ask the Holy Spirit who indwells me to effect
the will of the Lord Jesus Christ concerning these
afflicting powers of darkness. Just as You forced them
out of people's lives in response to Jesus' commands
when He walked the earth, I ask You to accomplish
that for me now. I ask You, Spirit of the living God,
to evict from my conscious, subconscious, and unconscious mind all control by any wicked powers. Break
all their ability to manipulate my thought processes.
They must go where the Lord Jesus Christ sends
them. Sweep them away and clear my mind of any
wicked spirit's dominion. I ask the Holy Spirit to
renew and sanctify my mind. Cleanse and take full
possession of my conscious, unconscious, and subcon-*

scious mind, precious Holy Spirit. Set it totally apart for the glory of God and the service of my Lord Jesus Christ. I deliberately yield my mind to the lordship of Christ, the truth of God's Word, and the will of my heavenly Father.

I ask the Holy Spirit to examine my emotions on the conscious, subconscious, and unconscious level. Evict any controlling powers of darkness, and may the holy angels escort them to the place where the Lord Jesus Christ commands them to go. Cleanse me of them. Totally remove them from me. I ask the gracious Holy Spirit to take control of my emotions on every level. Sanctify my emotions. Fill my emotions with the Spirit's fruit of love, joy, peace, patience, gentleness, kindness, goodness, faithfulness, and self-control. I welcome the Holy Spirit's internal control of my emotions. I look to the Spirit of God to sanctify and renew them. I gladly receive the Lord's plan for my emotional freedom and spiritual well-being.

I ask that the Holy Spirit search my conscious, unconscious, and subconscious will for any control by wicked powers. Evict them now to where the Lord Jesus Christ is commanding them to go. Sweep my mind clean of evil control and manipulation. May the Holy Spirit of the true and living God fully renew and sanctify my will for the glory of God. Place in me the desire to do God's perfect will so I might obediently and daily display the lordship of Jesus Christ in my life as the Holy Spirit controls my will.

I offer my entire body in all its functions as an act of spiritual worship to my heavenly Father. I ask the Holy Spirit to look throughout my body for any controlling activity of wicked spirits. Scan my brain and central nervous system for any fallen spirit's affliction or control. Evict them from this physical control center for the functions of my mind and body. I offer my brain and its capacities for the quickening, renewing control of the Holy Spirit. Sanctify and refresh my brain so that it functions in spiritual harmony with Your control of my whole person. Look all through my body and sever any control of my senses of vision, hearing, smell, touch, or taste by evil spirits. Carefully examine the organs of my body for any defiling work of the kingdom of darkness. Sanctify my body's organs and their function by the quickening work of the Holy Spirit.

I surrender all my physical appetites to Your lordship. I yield to You my need and craving for food and drink. Examine and cleanse from demonic activity all the organs of my digestive system. Set apart my sexuality for the glory of God. Evict any work of the Enemy in my sexual functions and organs. I surrender all these to Your lordship, and I submit myself to Your holy plan for moral purity and sexual intimacy within the bond of marriage.

Evict any afflicting, evil powers from every part of my body. Sanctify it in its entirety. I want my body to be holy, not just in its standing within God's redemptive plan, but also in its function. As a part of my spiritual worship to my Father in heaven, I offer my body as a living sacrifice for His use alone and for all that is acceptable in His sight.

I once again yield my whole person to the full control of the true and living God. I ask the Father, Son, and Holy Spirit to control me fully. I thank You for the freedom that You have effected within me during this time of prayer. I now look to the love of my heavenly Father, the lordship of Jesus Christ, and the ministry of the Holy Spirit to enable me daily to walk in the spiritual freedom promised to me in His Word. I reject, resist, and refuse anything less. In the name and worthiness of my Lord Jesus Christ and by the intercessions of the Holy Spirit, I place these petitions before my Father in heaven.

Additional Resources

Here are a variety of resources, including books and videos, that promote a child's security and thus help him or her overcome the Adversary. The resources cover five areas: building a loving marriage; communicating biblical sexual values; modeling the responsible use of money; giving a balanced, biblical view of spiritual warfare issues; and understanding how to rear your children.

BUILDING A LOVING MARRIAGE

Campbell, D. Ross. *How to Really Love Your Child.* Colorado Springs: Life Journey, Cook Communications, 2003.

Chapman, Gary. *The Five Love Languages.* Chicago: Moody Press, 1996.

Finzel, Hans, and Donna Finzel. *The Top Ten Ways to Love Your Wife.* Colorado Springs: Cook Communications, 2002.

Harley, Jr., Willard F. *His Needs, Her Needs.* Grand Rapids, MI: Revell, 1994.

McDowell, Josh, and Dick Day. *How to Be a Hero to Your Kids*. Dallas: Word, 1991.

Vezey, Denise. *Sizzle!* Colorado Springs: Life Journey, Cook Communications, 2006.

COMMUNICATING BIBLICAL SEXUAL VALUES

God's Design for Sex Series. Colorado Springs: NavPress, 1994. The four books in this series are titled *The Story of Me*, by Stan and Brenna Jones; *Before I Was Born*, by Carolyn Nystrom; *What's the Big Deal*, by Stan and Brenna Jones; and *Facing the Facts*, by Stan and Brenna Jones.

Learning about Sex Series. St. Louis, MO: Concordia Publishing House, 1998. This series is available in book and video form with helpful discussion sheets and leaders notes. The five books/videos, which are age graded, are titled *Why Boys and Girls Are Different* (ages 3–5), by Carol Greene; *Where Do Babies Come From?* (ages 6–8), by Ruth Hummel; *How You Are Changing* (ages 8–11), by Jane Graver; *Sex and the New You* (ages 11–14), by Richard Bimler; and *Love, Sex & God* (ages 14 and up), by Bill Ameiss and Jane Graver.

Scherrer, David L. and Linda M. Klepacki. *How to Talk to Your Kids About Sexuality*. Colorado Springs: Life Journey, Cook Communications, 2004.

MODELING THE RESPONSIBLE USE OF MONEY

Blue, Ron. *The New Master Your Money*. Chicago: Moody Press, 2004.

Briles, Judith. *Money Smarts*. Denver: Mile High Press, 2005.

Burkett, Larry. *The Family Financial Workbook*. Chicago: Moody Press, 2002.

Palmer, Scott, and Bethany Palmer. *Cents and Sensibility*. Colorado Springs: Life Journey, Cook Communications, 2005.

Crown Financial Ministries provides a wealth of materials that promote the biblical perspective on financial matters. You can contact them at Crown Financial Ministries, P.O. Box 100, Gainesville, GA 30503; 1-800-722-1976; www.crown.org.

GIVING A BALANCED, BIBLICAL VIEW OF SPIRITUAL WARFARE ISSUES

Anderson, Neil T. *Victory over the Darkness*. Ventura, CA: Regal, 2000.

Bubeck, Mark I. *The Adversary*. Chicago: Moody Press, 1975.

Dickason, Fred C. *Angels, Elect and Evil*. Chicago: Moody Press, 1995.

Logan, Jim. *Reclaiming Surrendered Ground: Protecting Your Family from Spiritual Attacks*. Chicago: Moody Press, 1995.

Murphy, Ed. *The Handbook for Spiritual Warfare* (rev. ed.). Nashville: Nelson, 2003.

Warner, Timothy M. *Spiritual Warfare*. Wheaton, IL: Crossway, 1991.

Wiersbe, Warren W. *The Strategy of Satan*. Wheaton, IL: Tyndale House, 1985.

UNDERSTANDING HOW TO REAR OUR CHILDREN

Campbell, D. Ross. *How to Really Love Your Angry Child*. Colorado Springs: Life Journey, Cook Communications, 2004.

Dobson, Dr. James. *Parenting Isn't for Cowards*. Sisters, OR: Multnomah, 2004.

———. *The New Dare to Discipline*. Wheaton, IL: Tyndale House, 1992.

Rogers, Adrian. *Ten Secrets for a Successful Family*. Wheaton, IL: Crossway, 1996.

Turansky, Scott, and Joanne Miller. *Parenting Is Heart Work*. Colorado Springs: Life Journey, Cook Communications, 2005.

Wright, Dr. H. Norman, and Gary J. Oliver. *Helping Your Kids Deal with Anger, Fear, and Sadness*. Eugene, OR: Harvest House, 2005.

Notes

CHAPTER 2: THE PRINCIPLE OF GENERATIONAL TRANSFER

1. Timothy M. Warner, *Spiritual Warfare* (Wheaton, IL: Crossway, 1991), 107.
2. G. Campbell Morgan, *The Westminster Pulpit*, vol. 4 (London: Pickering & Inglis, n.d.), 50.
3. Ed Murphy, *The Handbook for Spiritual Warfare* (Nashville: Thomas Nelson, 1992), 437–38.
4. C. Fred Dickason, *Demon Possession and the Christian*, (Wheaton, IL: Crossway, 1989), 221.
5. Mark I. Bubeck, *Overcoming the Adversary* (Chicago: Moody Press, 1984), 29–30.

CHAPTER 4: PARENTS WHO LOVE EACH OTHER

1. Ross Campbell, *How to Really Love Your Child* (Wheaton, IL: Victor, 1977), 22, 32.
2. Josh McDowell and Dick Day, *How to Be a Hero to Your Kids* (Dallas: Word, 1991), 9.

3. Ibid., 10–11.

4. Ibid., 11.

5. If you need help in developing "clear the air" times, consider a weekend Marriage Encounter retreat Contact them at 1-800-795-LOVE or go to wwme.org. Family Life Today also has a helpful marriage retreat called A Weekend to Remember. Contact them at 1-800-FLTODAY or go to familylife.com.

Chapter 5: Parents Who Communicate

1. Mark I. Bubeck, *The Adversary* (Chicago: Moody Press, 1975), 117–22.

2. A resource that can facilitate communication with your children on the issue of music is *Sex, Lies, and the Media* by Eva Marie and Jessica Everson (Colorado Springs: Life Journey, Cook Communications, 2005).

Chapter 6: Setting Our Children Free

* *For an in-depth presentation of how the Devil uses various outside arenas to threaten our spirit and soul, consult the video presentation "Interfacing Our Three Enemies," from the International Center for Biblical Counseling (ICBC), 1551 Indian Hills Dr., Suite 200, Sioux City, IA 51104. The ICBC also has several audio series on Satan's influence on our lives. Write ICBC for a complete catalog.*

Chapter 8: Preventing Demonic Harassment

* *Jehovah Nissi* means "God is my banner."

CHAPTER 9: SPIRITISTIC ACTIVITY IN CHILDREN

1. For an in-depth look at the ministries of angels, both good and evil, see C. Fred Dickason, *Angels, Elect and Evil* (Chicago: Moody, 1975).

2. Two books that are very helpful in understanding occult and satanic symbols and other clues to a child's interest in supernatural evil are: Johanna Michaelsen, *Like Lambs to the Slaughter* (Eugene, OR: Harvest House, 1989); and Anderson and Russo, *The Seduction of Our Children* (Eugene, OR: Harvest House, 1991).

READERS' GUIDE

*For Personal Reflection
or Group Discussion*

Readers' Guide

Nothing is more important to us as Christian parents than the spiritual well-being of our children. These precious lives are entrusted to us by God, and we are called to guide and protect them spiritually as well as physically. We know there is an Adversary who seeks to kill and destroy, who desires to hinder our children from becoming all God wants them to be. Yet our God, who loves them more than we do, has provided us with the tools we need to ensure our children can stand strong in the midst of spiritual attacks. This book can help you learn what those tools are and how to use them. The training takes discipline and hard work. But as we learn to face Satan's attacks for ourselves, to fight on behalf of our children, and to train our kids to stand strong on their own, we find that the battle has already been won.

The following questions are intended as a guide to help you think through some of the important issues raised in this book. They will help you start using the tools God has given to us. As you go through the guide, you may want to delve more deeply into some of these questions. Other questions may seem irrelevant to your situation. That's expected, as everyone's experiences differ. Simply allow the issues raised to inspire your thoughts. Also, don't rush through this guide. Often there aren't easy answers. Think through your responses and reflect on them awhile. While immediate answers may come to mind, the conclusions you reach after additional thought may prove to be the most beneficial.

This book and the following questions delve into issues that may be painful for some. If you find yourself in that situation, you may find it helpful to work through the book and study guide with a group of friends or like-minded parents. You also may find it necessary to seek out the guidance of a trusted pastor or counselor. Don't be afraid to do so. Working through the issues you face is an important step in teaching your children to walk in victory. The questions that follow may be a starting point in that process.

As you begin to enter the battle for your family's spiritual well-being, proceed with confidence. God will guide and empower you each step of the way. You may need to exercise patience, as sometimes ground is reclaimed slowly. But you'll begin to see God working powerfully and marvelously in your family's life as you overcome the Adversary at home.

CHAPTER 1: FOOTPRINTS IN THE CARPET

1. What is generational sin? Discuss whether it is possible for sins to impact just the individual committing them.

2. What are some of the main ways Satan can attack a family and introduce generational sins? Explain some of the more subtle ways Satan can influence a family.

3. A parent's influence impacts children for generations to come. This can be encouraging when it refers to a positive influence. In what ways can parents positively influence the spiritual lives of future generations? How can parents strengthen these positive influences in their family life?

4. What hinders believers from addressing generational sins in their lives? What does it take to overcome those barriers and end the cycle? What hinders believers from positive spiritual activity, such as focused time praying for their children? How can those barriers be overcome?

5. What generational sins have your family faced? How can you begin to break that trend? If you aren't sure, who will you ask for guidance?

6. What positive spiritual influences can you find in your family? List some ways they can be continued in the lives of your children. Pick one or two and determine how you will include them in your family life.

CHAPTER 2: THE PRINCIPLE OF GENERATIONAL TRANSFER

1. Explain the concept of generational transfer. How is God's redemptive grace the cure for generational sin? How does this grace offer hope when such sins seem so difficult to break?

2. Parents or other relatives often pass generational sins on to their children. With that in mind, how much of our sin is our personal responsibility and how much is a result of our past?

3. What are the three major things a parent can do that might open up a child to Satan's influence? Have you seen any of these at work in your life or in someone else's? How did it impact your life or your friend's?

4. What generational sins do you struggle to avoid? What makes them difficult to break? In contrast, who in your family is a positive spiritual warrior? How can you begin to learn from that person's example?

5. What weapons does God give us to overcome Satan's attacks? Why don't we use them more often? What will you do to sharpen your ability in using them?

CHAPTER 3: PRAYERS THAT PARALYZE THE ADVERSARY

1. What are some specific qualities of prayer that can paralyze the Adversary? In what ways do your own prayers exhibit these qualities? How might these qualities be lacking?

2. Consider the various misconceptions we have about sin. Which of these do you find yourself believing? If we truly believe in God's forgiveness and in His goodness, why do we buy into these misconceptions?

3. What would you say to a friend who told you she believes she can't escape the generational sin in her family?

4. Of the three misconceptions about generational sin, which

misconception is the hardest for you to overcome? Why? What
steps can you take to begin to see things from God's perspective?

5. How have you seen God answer your prayers for your child in the
   past? Name specific areas in your child's life for which you will
   begin asking God to intervene.

6. Write your own generational prayers for your child(ren). Be specific in your requests before God.

CHAPTER 4: PARENTS WHO LOVE EACH OTHER

1. What barriers are there between you and your spouse? How have
   you addressed them? What will it take to break through those barriers? How can you begin to make that happen? Which of the
   "Other Ways to Increase Marital Love" might be helpful?

2. In what ways are you currently dedicating a portion of your
   income to the Lord? What areas of your finances are you afraid to
   allow God to control? Why? What step can you take today to grow
   more disciplined in your finances?

3. Are there certain circumstances that make communication between
   you and your spouse difficult? Are there specific issues that
   repeatedly cause problems? What can you do when these issues
   arise to stop fighting each other and begin to fight the real Enemy?

4. Set aside a specific time to pray for your marriage and family. If
   possible, make it a time you can pray with your spouse. Which of
   the four methods of prayer (fasting, daily, prevailing, and family)
   will work best for your situation? What areas of your marriage
   will you commit to pray for regularly?

5. Sexual intimacy is an important issue in marriage, but it is often difficult to discuss. How safe do you feel talking to your spouse about such issues? How safe do you make it for him or her to talk to you?

6. Name three ways you can put your spouse's needs before yours in this area of your relationship. Plan some fun ways you can help make that happen.

CHAPTER 5: PARENTS WHO COMMUNICATE

1. Nothing is more important than our children's salvation. What is your child's relationship with God like right now? How have you modeled your relationship with Christ to him or her? How can you begin to open up spiritual discussions with your child? List three spiritual issues you'd like to focus on in the coming months.

2. How do you currently express your love to your children? In what ways do you encourage them? What expressions of love do your children appreciate the most? Pick one of the listed ways to say I love you for each of your children. Commit to do that once each day for the next two weeks.

3. What kind of impact can a parent have on her child's perspective of sex? If a parent doesn't teach her child, where might the child learn about this topic? What will you do to help ensure your child feels comfortable talking to you about sex?

4. What do you know about the things your children have already learned about sex and the pressures they face in this area? Why are parents sometimes uninformed about this area of their child's life?

5. Why is it important to talk to children about the occult and other more subtle satanic influences? How can you discover more about what your children have learned about these topics from the media, their friends, and their schools?

6. How can you become more informed about your children's greatest influences—friends and school? List some ways you can get involved to ensure their schooling is a positive influence. How can you begin to get to know your children's friends better? List some ways you can help encourage friends who are good influences on your kids.

Chapter 6: Setting Our Children Free

1. What do you believe about your identity in Christ? Of the truths about your identity listed by the author, which do you struggle the most to believe? If your perspective about yourself is not how God sees you, how can you change your view to match His? How can you better model for and teach your children about a believer's identity in Christ?

2. God originally designed human beings without flaw. How was that perfection skewed in the fall? (Consider areas such as the spirit, soul, and body.)

3. In what ways do people still struggle with their fallen natures after salvation? More personally, in what ways do you struggle? Why do we struggle, even after we become children of God?

4. Are there things we can do ourselves to help overcome our fallen natures? What is our responsibility in this area and what is God's?

5. How does the new life we receive at salvation give us hope regarding our sinful natures? List some ways we are changed to be more like God intended.

6. Are there ways that understanding the fall and redemption can help us in dealing with our children's sin? How does it encourage more patience and understanding? On the other hand, how does it highlight parents' responsibility in helping their child overcome sin?

CHAPTER 7: LEARNING TO WALK IN FREEDOM

1. Take a moment just between you and God. What sin in your life do you find difficult to control? How have you sought to overcome it in the past? Have you made progress? Why or why not?

2. What do theologians mean by the term *total depravity?* Is there any area of an individual's life that hasn't been touched by sin? What evidence of total depravity have you seen in your life or in the lives of others?

3. When an area of life seems under control—or not so depraved—why might that be?

4. What is the difference between temptation and sin? Does God hold you accountable for things you are simply tempted to do? Is it easy to sense temptation before it leads to sin? What benefit is there when we are aware of a temptation before it leads to sin?

5. What are the three truths that can help us overcome sinful desires? Which is the hardest for you to believe? Why is it sometimes difficult to remember these truths when we are faced with temptation?

6. While parental discipline is important for children, why is it sometimes not enough to help their hearts overcome the sinful nature? What are some of the messages we send our children when we teach the "three truths"? What steps can you take to help your children understand these truths?

CHAPTER 8: PREVENTING DEMONIC HARASSMENT

1. Why is it so easy to indulge our sinful natures? What happens when we do? What kind of opening into our lives does this give Satan? How can honest confession and the recognition that we are "dead to Christ" help diminish sinful desires?

2. What is the first step in overcoming temptation? Why is it important to take this step for your own life before beginning to work on it with your children? What in your life makes this first step difficult to take? What can make it easier?

3. When following the examples of the resistance prayers in this chapter, will results be immediate? Why or why not? How have you seen persistent and patient prayer pay off in your life or in a friend's life?

4. How does understanding that Satan's kingdom is both structured and counterfeit help when a believer is fighting against it? What truths about the relationship between God's kingdom and Satan's kingdom give you hope in the battle?

5. Why is it difficult to recognize Satan's kingdom even though it is right in front of us? What steps can you take to better understand and recognize Satan's counterfeit family, gospels, ministers, righteousness, and worship?

6. How can knowing Satan's limits and understanding scriptural truth help parents understand and exert their parental authority? In what ways have you already exerted that authority on behalf of your child? In what areas would you like to reclaim that authority?

CHAPTER 9: SPIRITISTIC ACTIVITY IN CHILDREN

1. When considering spiritistic activity in our children, why is it important to discern between normal childhood behaviors and demonic influence? What can happen if a parent jumps to the conclusion that Satan is involved when he isn't?

2. Explain why parents must prayerfully consider their response when they sense that their child is under attack. What is a healthy, effective, and appropriate approach for parents when dealing with spiritistic activity in their children?

3. What should a parent's demeanor and attitude be when discussing possible spiritual activity with their children? What attitude should they strive to instill in their children?

4. The author presents five main evidences of spiritistic activity in children. How is each one a perversion of—even the very opposite of—the commands God gave His children?

5. What hopeful truths can we hold on to when our children are being spiritually influenced in a harmful way? Share or list some reasons why there is no need for fear—regardless of circumstances.

6. If you were to recognize spiritistic activity in your children, what would you say to them about it? When should you discuss it with them, and when should you not talk about it directly? How would

you explain the existence and activity of Satan in a way that illustrates the very real danger he poses but doesn't encourage undue fear in your child?

CHAPTER 10: APPLYING THE SEVEN STEPS TO FREEDOM

1. What lessons about generational influences struck you as you read the story of Manasseh? Was the state of Judah hopeless after he sinned so severely? If not, why? What similar stories of positive and negative influences are found in your own family?

2. Why is it important to renounce all past involvement with occultic and spiritistic activities, even those we barely remember? In what ways might a person be influenced without even being aware of it?

3. What makes it so difficult to admit you've been deceived about something, particularly spiritually? Which of the disciplines for combating deceit mentioned by the author will you begin today?

4. Our sinful nature often takes the form of wrong attitudes such as bitterness, rebellion, and pride.

   a. Why do people sometimes want to withhold forgiveness? When do you find it difficult to forgive and why?

   b. In what areas of your life are you tempted to rebel? Why do you find it difficult to submit in these areas?

   c. What are some of the ways pride can express itself in a person's life? Are these as dangerous or destructive as more subtle ways?

5. How have you allowed sins of the flesh to be a part of your life—either in the past or in the present? Are there ways these types of sins are more difficult to break, or are they like any other sin? What ways do you need to change your life to make resisting such sins easier?

6. What sin areas in your life can be attributed to generational transfer? Are there sins in your extended family that may not be affecting you personally but may influence future generations?

7. This whole chapter was focused on the parent and didn't directly involve the child. Why is it so vital for a believer to go through this prayer process if he or she is to lead a child to spiritual victory? What would you say to a friend if she felt guilty and thought it was too late to find freedom?

CHAPTER 11: PRAYER THAT DEFEATS THE RULE OF EVIL

1. Prayer seems like such a simple way to protect our children spiritually. What keeps you from believing it will work? What prevents you from investing time doing it? What areas of your life can you adjust to allow more opportunities for prayer?

2. As you consider Kevin's story, what clues told Sally that this was not an issue of imagination? What about Sally's response enabled her son to learn to confront demonic activity with confidence? If in a related situation, what would you do similarly to Sally? What might you do differently?

3. Why did it take Sally awhile to recognize that the conflict with Steve was spiritual? What is it about the "heat of battle" that makes this tough to see at the time? What did Sally do that transformed the situation, although not overnight? Describe the

changes both in Sally and Steve when she approached this from a spiritual perspective.

4. Why is it sometimes easier to forget the need for spiritual warfare prayer on behalf of children, such as Kelly, who don't seem to be struggling? In what ways can spiritual warfare prayer be used to bless our children as much as to protect them?

5. What insights about spiritual warfare did Sally gain from the situations with Kevin? With Steve? With Kelly? How can a mom—even a self-described "spiritual warfare mom"—expand her vision for the well-being of her children in the spiritual realm?

6. For each of your children, make a list of the struggles they are facing. Which of these areas might be due to a spiritual attack? What are some specific things you can pray to help the find victory? What one thing will you do today to begin teaching your children to stand strong for themselves in the face of the Enemy?